GREEK
TRAGEDIES

VOLUME 1

Edited by David Grene & Richmond Lattimore

THIRD EDITION *Edited by Mark Griffith & Glenn W. Most*

 VOLUME 1

The University of Chicago Press CHICAGO & LONDON

MARK GRIFFITH is professor of classics and
of theater, dance, and performance studies at
the University of California, Berkeley.

GLENN W. MOST is professor of ancient
Greek at the Scuola Normale Superiore at Pisa
and a visiting member of the Committee on
Social Thought at the University of Chicago.

DAVID GRENE (1913–2002) taught classics for
many years at the University of Chicago.

RICHMOND LATTIMORE (1906–1984),
professor of Greek at Bryn Mawr College,
was a poet and translator best known for his
translations of the Greek classics, especially his
versions of the *Iliad* and the *Odyssey*.

The University of Chicago Press, Chicago 60637
The University of Chicago Press, Ltd., London
© 2013 by The University of Chicago

Agamemnon © 1947 by Richmond Lattimore,
© 1953, 2013 by the University of Chicago
Prometheus Bound © 1942, 1991, 2013 by the
University of Chicago
Oedipus the King © 1942, 2013 by the University
of Chicago
Antigone © 1954, 2013 by the University of
Chicago
Hippolytus © 1942, 2013 by the University of
Chicago

27 26 25 24 23 22 21 20 19 18   6 7 8 9 10

ISBN-13: 978-0-226-03514-7 (cloth)
ISBN-13: 978-0-226-03528-4 (paper)
ISBN-13: 978-0-226-03531-4 (e-book)

Library of Congress Cataloging-in-Publication
Data

Greek tragedies / edited by David Grene and
Richmond Lattimore. — Third edition / edited
by Mark Griffith and Glenn W. Most.
  pages. cm.
    ISBN 978-0-226-03514-7 (cloth : alk. paper)
— ISBN 978-0-226-03528-4 (pbk. : alk. paper)
— ISBN 978-0-226-03531-4 (e-book) — ISBN
978-0-226-03545-1 (cloth : alk. paper) — ISBN
978-0-226-03559-8 (pbk. : alk. paper) — ISBN 978-
0-226-03562-8 (e-book) — ISBN 978-0-226-
03576-5 (cloth : alk. paper) — ISBN 978-0-
226-03593-2 (pbk. : alk. paper) — ISBN 978-0-
226-03609-0 (e-book) 1. Greek drama (Tragedy)
I. Grene, David. II. Lattimore, Richmond,
1906–1984. III. Wyckoff, Elizabeth, 1915– IV.
Most, Glenn W. V. Griffith, Mark (Classicist)
VI. Sophocles. Antigone. English. 2013. VII.
Sophocles. Oedipus Rex. English. 2013. VIII.
Aeschylus. Agamemnon. English. 2013. IX.
Aeschylus. Prometheus bound. English. 2013. X.
Euripides. Hippolytus. English. 2013.
    PA3626.A2G57 2013
    882'.0108—dc23

                                    2012044399

♾ This paper meets the requirements of ANSI/
NISO Z39.48-1992 (Permanence of Paper).

CONTENTS

AGAMEMNON

AESCHYLUS
Translated by Richmond Lattimore

INTRODUCTION TO
AESCHYLUS' AGAMEMNON

Agamemnon is the first part of the trilogy known as the *Oresteia*, the other two parts being *The Libation Bearers* and *The Eumenides*. The trilogy was presented in 458 BCE and won first prize.

According to the legend, in the version used by Aeschylus, Atreus tricked his brother, Thyestes, into devouring his own children, all but one. Thyestes cursed the entire house. In the next generation, Agamemnon and Menelaus, sons of Atreus, were kings in Argos. Helen, wife of Menelaus, eloped to Troy with Paris (Alexander). Agamemnon led the expedition to Troy to recover her, and, to procure favorable winds to get there, sacrificed his daughter, Iphigeneia, to Artemis. Meanwhile Agamemnon's wife Clytaemestra took as her lover Aegisthus, the only surviving son of Thyestes. Agamemnon and Clytaemestra arranged a series of beacons between Argos and Troy, by which he would signal the capture of the city.

It is at this point that *Agamemnon* begins. The action consists of a short, simple series of events: the return of Agamemnon with his captured war prize, Cassandra; his formal reception and entrance into the palace; the murder of Agamemnon and Cassandra by Clytaemestra and Aegisthus; and, at the end, their defiance of Argos and its citizens. The power of the drama lies partly in the arrangement of these events, partly also in the choral lyrics and long speeches, in which the tragic scenes of the past, flashbacks in memory, as well as hints about the future, are made to enlarge and illuminate the action and persons before us.

AGAMEMNON

Characters   WATCHMAN
CHORUS of Argive Elders
CLYTAEMESTRA, wife of Agamemnon
HERALD
AGAMEMNON, son of Atreus and king of Argos
CASSANDRA, daughter of King Priam of Troy
AEGISTHUS, cousin of Agamemnon

*Scene: Argos, in front of the palace of King Agamemnon. The
Watchman is posted on the roof.*

WATCHMAN
I ask the gods some respite from the weariness
of this watchtime measured by years I lie awake
elbowed upon the Atreidae's roof dogwise to mark
the grand processionals of all the stars of night
burdened with winter and again with heat for men,   5
dynasties in their shining blazoned on the air,
these stars, upon their wane and when the rest arise.
I wait; to read the meaning in that beacon light,
a blaze of fire to carry out of Troy the rumor
and outcry of its capture; to such end a lady's   10
male strength of heart in its high confidence ordains.
Now as this bed stricken with night and drenched with dew
I keep, nor ever with kind dreams for company—
since fear in sleep's place stands forever at my head
against strong closure of my eyes, or any rest—   15

I mince such medicine against sleep failed: I sing,
only to weep again the pity of this house
no longer, as once, administered in the grand way.
Now let there be again redemption from distress,
the flare burning from the blackness in good augury.   20

(A light shows in the distance.)

Oh hail, blaze of the darkness, harbinger of day's
shining, and of processionals and dance and songs
of multitudes in Argos for this day of thanks.
Ho there, ho!
I cry the news aloud to Agamemnon's queen,   25
that she may rise up from her bed of state with speed
to raise the rumor of gladness welcoming this beacon,
and singing rise, if truly the citadel of Ilium
has fallen, as the shining of this flare proclaims.
I also, I, will make my choral prelude, since   30
my lord's dice cast aright are counted as my own,
and mine the tripled sixes of this torchlit throw.
May it only happen. May my king come home, and I
take up within this hand the hand I love. The rest
I leave to silence; for an ox stands huge upon   35
my tongue. The house itself, could it take voice, might speak
aloud and plain. I speak to those who understand,
but if they fail, I have forgotten everything.

(Exit. Enter the Chorus from the side.)

CHORUS [chanting]
  Ten years since the great contestants   40
  of Priam's right,
  Menelaus and Agamemnon, my lord,
  twin throned, twin sceptered, in twofold power
  of kings from god, the Atreidae,
  put forth from this shore   45
  the thousand ships of the Argives,
  the strength and the armies.

Their cry of war went shrill from the heart,
as eagles stricken in agony
for young perished, high from the nest   50
eddy and circle
to bend and sweep of the wings' stroke,
lost far below
the fledglings, the nest, and the tendance.
Yet someone hears in the air, a god,   55
Apollo, Pan, or Zeus, the high
thin wail of these sky-guests, and drives
late to its mark
the Fury upon the transgressors.

So drives Zeus, the great god of guests,   60
the Atreidae against Alexander:
for one woman's promiscuous sake
the struggling masses, legs tired,
knees grinding in dust,
spears broken in the onset.   65
Danaans and Trojans
they have it alike. It goes as it goes
now. The end will be destiny.
You cannot burn flesh or pour unguents,
not innocent cool tears,°   70
that will soften the gods' stiff anger.
But we, dishonored, old in our bones,
cast off even then from the gathering horde,
stay here, to prop up
on staves the strength of a baby.   75
Since the young vigor that urges
inward to the heart
is frail as age, no warcraft yet perfect,
while beyond age, leaf
withered, man goes three-footed   80
no stronger than a child is,
a dream that falters in daylight.°

But you, lady,
daughter of Tyndareus, Clytaemestra, our queen:
What is there to be done? What new thing have you heard? 85
In persuasion of what
report do you order such sacrifice?
To all the gods of the city,
the high and the deep spirits,
to them of the sky and the marketplaces, 90
the altars blaze with oblations.
The staggered flame goes sky-high
one place, then another,
drugged by the simple soft
persuasion of sacred unguents, 95
the deep-stored oil of the kings.
Of these things what can be told
openly, speak.
Be healer to this perplexity
that grows now into darkness of thought, 100
while again sweet hope shining from the flames
beats back the pitiless pondering
of sorrow that eats my heart.

[*singing*]

STROPHE A

I have mastery yet to proclaim the wonder at the wayside
given to kings. Still by god's grace there surges within me 105
singing magic
grown to my life and power,
how the wild bird portent
hurled forth the Achaeans'
twin-stemmed power single-hearted, 110
lords of the youth of Hellas,
with spear and hand of strength
to the land of Teucrus.
Kings of birds to the kings of the ships,

one black, one blazed with silver,   115
clear seen by the royal house
on the right, the spear hand,
they alighted, watched by all
tore a hare, ripe, bursting with young unborn yet,
stayed from her last fleet running.   120
  Sing sorrow, sorrow: but good win out in the end.

ANTISTROPHE A

Then the grave seer of the host saw through to the hearts divided,
knew the fighting sons of Atreus feeding on the hare
with the host, their people.
Seeing beyond, he spoke: 125
"With time, this foray
shall stalk the city of Priam;
and under the walls, Fate shall spoil
in violence the rich herds of the people.   130
Only let no doom of the gods darken
upon this huge iron forged to curb Troy—
from inward. Artemis the undefiled
is angered with pity
at the flying hounds of her father   135
eating the unborn young in the hare and the shivering mother.
She is sick at the eagles' feasting.
  Sing sorrow, sorrow: but good win out in the end.

EPODE

Lovely she is and kind   140
to the tender young of ravening lions.
For sucklings of all the savage
beasts that lurk in the lonely places she has sympathy.
She demands meaning° for these appearances
good, yet not without evil.   145
Healer Apollo, I pray you
let her not with crosswinds
bind the ships of the Danaans

to time-long anchorage   150
forcing a second sacrifice unholy, untasted,
working bitterness in the blood and fearing no man.
For the terror returns like sickness to lurk in the house;
the secret anger remembers the child that shall be avenged."   155
Such, with great good things beside, rang out in the voice of
   Calchas,
these fatal signs from the birds by the way to the house of the
   princes,
wherewith in sympathy
   sing sorrow, sorrow: but good win out in the end.

STROPHE B

Zeus: whatever he may be, if this name   160
pleases him in invocation,
thus I call upon him.
I have pondered everything
yet I cannot find a way,
only Zeus, to cast this dead weight of ignorance   165
finally from out my brain.

ANTISTROPHE B

He who in time long ago was great,
throbbing with gigantic strength,
shall be as if he never were, unspoken.   170
He who followed him has found
his master, and is gone.
Cry aloud without fear the victory of Zeus;
you will not have failed the truth.   175

STROPHE C

Zeus, who guided men to think,
who has laid it down that wisdom
comes alone through suffering.
Still there drips in sleep against the heart
grief of memory; against   180

our will temperance comes.
From the gods who sit in grandeur
grace is somehow violent.

ANTISTROPHE C

On that day the elder king
of the Achaean ships, not faulting
any prophet's word,   185
shifted with the crosswinds of fortune,
when no ship sailed, no pail was full,
and the Achaean people sulked
along the shore at Aulis facing
Chalcis, where tides ebb and surge: 190

STROPHE D

and winds blew from the Strymon, bearing
sick idleness, ships tied fast, and hunger,
distraction of the mind, carelessness
for hull and cable;   195
with time's length bent to double measure
by delay crumbled the flower and pride
of Argos. Then against the bitter wind
the seer's voice clashed out
another medicine   200
more hateful yet, and spoke of Artemis, so that the kings
dashed their staves to the ground and could not hold their tears.

ANTISTROPHE D

The elder lord spoke aloud before them: 205
"My fate is angry if I disobey these,
but angry if I slaughter
this child, the beauty of my house,
with maiden bloodshed staining
these father's hands beside the altar.   210
What of these things goes now without disaster?
How shall I fail my ships

and lose my faith of battle?
To urge the wind-changing sacrifice of maiden's blood   215
angrily, for the wrath is great—it is right.° May all be well yet."

STROPHE E
But when he put on necessity's yoke
he changed, and from the heart the breath came bitter
and sacrilegious, utterly infidel,   220
to warp a will now to be stopped at nothing.
The sickening in men's minds, mad,
reckless in first cruelty brings daring. He endured then
to sacrifice his daughter
in support of war waged for a woman,   225
first offering for the ships' sake.

ANTISTROPHE E
Her supplications and her cries of father
were nothing, nor the child's lamentation
to kings passioned for battle.   230
The father prayed, called to his men to lift her
with strength of hand swept in her robes aloft
and prone above the altar, as you might lift
a goat for sacrifice—with a guard
against the lips' sweet edge, to check   235
the curse cried on the house of Atreus
by force and a bit's speechless power.

STROPHE F
Pouring then to the ground her saffron mantle
she struck the sacrificers with   240
the eyes' arrows of pity,
lovely as in a painted scene, and striving
to speak—as many times
at the kind festive table of her father
she had sung, and in the clear voice of a stainless maiden   245
with love had graced the song
of worship when the third cup was poured.

What happened next I saw not, neither speak it.
The crafts of Calchas fail not of outcome.
Justice tilts her scale so that those only   250
learn who suffer; and the future
you shall know when it has come; before then, forget it.
It is grief too soon given.
All will come clear in the next dawn's sunlight.
Let good fortune follow these things as   255
the one who is here desires,
our Apian land's single-hearted protector.°

(Enter Clytaemestra.)

CHORUS LEADER
   I have come in reverence, Clytaemestra, of your power.
   For when the man is gone and the throne void, his right
   falls to the prince's lady, and honor must be given.   260
   Is it some grace—or otherwise—that you have heard
   to make you sacrifice at messages of good hope?
   I should be glad to hear, but must not blame your silence.

CLYTAEMESTRA
   As it was said of old, may the dawn child be born
   to be an angel of blessing from the kindly night.   265
   You shall know joy beyond all you ever hoped to hear.
   The men of Argos have taken Priam's citadel.

CHORUS LEADER
   What have you said? Your words escaped my doubting mind.

CLYTAEMESTRA
   The Achaeans are in Troy. Is that not clear enough?

CHORUS LEADER
   This slow delight steals over me to bring forth tears.   270

CLYTAEMESTRA
   Yes, for your eyes betray the loyal heart within.

CHORUS LEADER

Yet how can I be certain? Is there some evidence?

CLYTAEMESTRA

There is, there must be; unless a god has lied to me.

CHORUS LEADER

Is it dream visions, easy to believe, you credit?

CLYTAEMESTRA

I accept nothing from a brain that is dull with sleep.   275

CHORUS LEADER

The charm, then, of some rumor, that made rich your hope?

CLYTAEMESTRA

Am I some young girl, that you find my thoughts so silly?

CHORUS LEADER

How long, then, is it since the citadel was stormed?

CLYTAEMESTRA

It was the night, the mother of this dawn I hailed.

CHORUS LEADER

What kind of messenger could come in speed like this?   280

CLYTAEMESTRA

Hephaestus, who cast forth the shining blaze from Ida.
And beacon after beacon picking up the flare
carried it here; Ida to the Hermaean horn
of Lemnos, where it shone above the isle, and next
the sheer rock face of Zeus on Athos caught it up;   285
and plunging skyward to arch the shoulders of the sea
the strength of the running flare in exultation,°
pine timbers flaming into gold, like the sunrise,
brought the bright message to Macistus' sentinel cliffs,
who, never slow nor in the carelessness of sleep   290
caught up, sent on his relay in the courier chain,
and far across Euripus' streams the beacon flare

carried to signal watchmen on Messapion.
These took it again in turn, and heaping high a pile
of silvery brush flamed it to throw the message on.   295
And the flare sickened never, but grown stronger yet
outleapt the river valley of Asopus like
the very moon for shining, to Cithaeron's scaur
to waken the next station of the flaming post.
These watchers, not contemptuous of the far-thrown blaze,   300
kindled another beacon vaster than commanded.
The light leaned high above Gorgopis' staring marsh,
and striking Aegyplanctus' mountaintop, drove on
yet one more relay, lest the flare die down in speed.
Kindled once more with stintless heaping force, they send   305
the beard of flame to hugeness, passing far beyond
the promontory that gazes on the Saronic strait
and flaming far, until it plunged at last to strike
the steep rock of Arachnus near at hand, our watchtower.
And thence there fell upon this house of Atreus' sons   310
the flare whose fathers mount to the Idaean beacon.
These are the changes on my torchlight messengers,
one from another running out the laps assigned.
The first and the last sprinters have the victory.
By such proof and such symbol I announce to you   315
my lord at Troy has sent his messengers to me.

CHORUS LEADER

The gods, lady, shall have my prayers and thanks straightway.
And yet to hear your story till all wonder fades
would be my wish, could you but tell it once again.

CLYTAEMESTRA

The Achaeans have got Troy, upon this very day.   320
I think the city echoes with a clash of cries.
Pour vinegar and oil into the selfsame bowl,
you could not say they mix in friendship, but fight on.
Thus variant sound the voices of the conquerors
and conquered, from the opposition of their fates.   325

Trojans are stooping now to gather in their arms
their dead, husbands and brothers; children lean to clasp
the aged who begot them, crying upon the death
of those most dear, from lips that never will be free.
The Achaeans have their midnight work after the fighting   330
that sets them down to feed on all the city has,
ravenous, headlong, by no rank and file assigned,
but as each man has drawn his shaken lot by chance.
And in the Trojan houses that their spears have taken
they settle now, free of the open sky, the frosts   335
and dampness of the evening; without sentinels set
they sleep the sleep of happiness the whole night through.
And if they reverence the gods who hold the city
and all the holy temples of the captured land,
they, the despoilers, might not be despoiled in turn.   340
Let not their passion overwhelm them; let no lust
seize on these men to violate what they must not.
The run to safety and home is yet to make; they must turn
the post, and run the backstretch of the double course.
Yet, though the host come home without offence to high   345
gods, even so the anger of these slaughtered men
may never sleep. Oh, let there be no fresh wrong done!
Such are the thoughts you hear from me, a woman merely.
Yet may the best win through, that none may fail to see.
Of all good things to wish this is my dearest choice.   350

CHORUS LEADER
My lady, you speak graciously like a prudent man.
I have listened to the proofs of your tale, and I believe,
and go to make my glad thanksgivings to the gods.
This pleasure is not unworthy of the grief that gave it.

(*Exit Clytaemestra into the palace.*)

[*chanting*]
O Zeus our lord and Night beloved,   355
bestower of power and beauty,

you slung above the bastions of Troy
the binding net, that none, neither great
nor young, might outleap
the gigantic toils   360
of enslavement and final disaster.
I gaze in awe on Zeus of the guests
who wrung from Alexander such payment.
He bent the bow with slow care, that neither
the shaft might hurdle the stars, nor fall   365
spent to the earth, short driven.

[*singing*]

STROPHE A

They have the stroke of Zeus to tell of.
This thing is clear and you may trace it.
He acted as he had decreed. A man thought
the gods deigned not to punish mortals   370
who trampled down the delicacy of things
inviolable. That man was wicked.
The curse on great daring
shines clear; it wrings atonement   375
from those high hearts that drive to evil,
from houses blossoming to pride
and peril. Let there be
wealth without tears; enough for
the wise man who will ask no further.   380
There is not any armor
in riches against perdition
for him who kicks the high altar
of Justice down to the darkness.

ANTISTROPHE A

Persuasion the persistent overwhelms him,   385
she, strong daughter of designing Ruin.
And every medicine is vain; the sin
smolders not, but burns to evil beauty.
As worthless bronze rubbed   390

at the touchstone relapses
to blackness and grime, so this man
tested shows vain
as a child that strives to catch the bird flying
and wins shame that shall bring down his city.   395
No god will hear such a man's entreaty,
but whoever turns to these ways
they strike him down in his wickedness.
This was Paris: he came
to the house of the sons of Atreus,   400
stole the woman away, and shamed
the guest's right of the board shared.

STROPHE B

She left among her people the stir and clamor
of shields and of spearheads,   405
the ships to sail and the armor.
She took to Ilium her dowry, death.
She stepped forth lightly between the gates
daring beyond all daring. And the prophets
about the great house wept aloud and spoke:
"Alas, alas for the house and for the champions,   410
alas for the bed signed with their love together.
Here now is silence, scorned, unreproachful.
The agony of his loss is clear before us.
Longing for her who lies beyond the sea
he shall see a phantom queen in his household.   415
Her images in their beauty
are bitterness to her lord now
where in the emptiness of eyes
all passion has faded."

ANTISTROPHE B

Shining in dreams the sorrowful   420
memories pass; they bring him
vain delight only.
It is vain, to dream and to see splendors,

and the image slipping from the arms' embrace
escapes, not to return again,   425
on wings drifting down the ways of sleep.
Such have the sorrows been in the house by the hearthside;
such have there been, and yet there are worse than these.
In all Hellas, for those who swarmed to the war,
the heartbreaking misery   430
shows in the house of each.
Many are they who are touched at the heart by these things.
Those they sent forth they knew;
now, in place of the young men
urns and ashes are carried home   435
to the houses of the fighters.

STROPHE C

The god of war, money changer of dead bodies,
held the balance of his spear in the fighting,
and from the corpse-fires at Ilium   440
sent to their dearest the dust
heavy and bitter with tears shed
packing smooth the urns with
ashes that once were men.
They praise them through their tears, how this man   445
knew well the craft of battle, how another
went down splendid in the slaughter:
and all for someone else's woman.
Thus they mutter in secrecy,
and the slow anger creeps below their grief   450
at Atreus' sons and their quarrels.
There by the walls of Ilium
the young men in their beauty keep
graves deep in the alien soil
they hated and they conquered.   455

ANTISTROPHE C

The citizens speak: their voice is deep with hatred.
The curse of the people must be paid for.

[19] AGAMEMNON

There lurks for me in the hooded night
terror of what may be told me.   460
The gods fail not to note
those who have killed many.
The black Furies, stalking the man
fortunate but without justice,
wrench back again the set of his life   465
and drop him to darkness. There among
the ciphers there is no more comfort
in power. And the vaunt of high glory
is bitterness; for god's thunderbolts
crash on the towering houses.°   470
Let me attain no envied wealth;
let me not plunder cities,
neither be captured in turn, and face
life in the power of another.

                            EPODE

From the beacon's bright message   475
the swift rumor runs
through the city. If this be real
who knows? Perhaps the gods have sent some lie to us.
    —Who of us is so childish or so short of wit
that by the beacon's messages   480
his heart flamed must sink down again
when the tale changes in the end?
    —It is like a woman indeed
to take the rapture before the fact has shown for true.
    Women believe too easily, are too quick to shift   485
from ground to ground; and swift indeed
the rumor voiced by a woman dies again.

CHORUS LEADER
  Now we° shall understand these torches and their shining,
  the beacons, and the interchange of flame and flame.   490
  They may be real; yet bright and dreamwise ecstasy
  in light's appearance might have charmed our hearts awry.

I see a herald coming from the beach, his brows
shaded with sprigs of olive; and upon his feet
the dust, dry sister of the mud, makes plain to me   495
that he will find a voice, not merely kindle flame
from mountain timber, and make signals from the smoke,
but tell us outright, whether to be happy, or—
but I shrink back from naming the alternative.
That which appeared was good; may yet more good be given.   500

And any man who prays that different things befall
the city, may he reap the crime of his own heart.

(Enter the Herald from the side.)

HERALD
Soil of my fathers, Argive earth I tread upon,
in daylight of the tenth year I have come back to you.
All my hopes broke but one, and this I have at last.   505
I never could have dared to dream that I might die
in Argos, and be buried in this beloved soil.
Hail to the Argive land and to its sunlight; hail
to its high sovereign, Zeus, and to the Pythian king.
May you no longer shower your arrows on our heads.   510
Beside Scamandrus you were grim; be satisfied
and turn to savior now and healer of our hurts,
my lord Apollo. Gods of the marketplace assembled,
I greet you all, and my own patron deity
Hermes, beloved herald, in whose right all heralds   515
are sacred; and you heroes that sent forth the host,
propitiously take back all that the spear has left.
O great hall of the kings and house beloved; seats
of sanctity; divinities that face the sun:
if ever before, look now with kind and glowing eyes   520
to greet our king in state after so long a time.
He comes, Lord Agamemnon, bearing light in gloom
to you, and to all that are assembled here.
Salute him with good favor, as he well deserves,
the man who has wrecked Ilium with the spade of Zeus   525

vindictive, whereby all their plain has been laid waste.
Gone are their altars; the sacred places of the gods
are gone, and scattered all the seed within the ground.
With such a yoke as this gripped to the neck of Troy
he comes, the king, Atreus' elder son, a man   530
fortunate to be honored far above all men
alive; not Paris nor the city tied to him
can boast he did more than was done him in return.
Guilty of rape and theft, condemned, he lost the prize
captured, and broke to sheer destruction all the house   535
of his fathers, with the very ground whereon it stood.
Twice over the sons of Priam have atoned their sins.

CHORUS LEADER
Hail and be glad, herald of the Achaean host.

HERALD
I am happy; I no longer ask the gods for death.

CHORUS LEADER
Did passion for your country so strip bare your heart?   540

HERALD
So that the tears broke in my eyes, for happiness.

CHORUS LEADER
You were taken with that sickness, then, that brings delight.

HERALD
How? I cannot deal with such words until I understand.

CHORUS LEADER
Struck with desire of those who loved as much again.

HERALD
You mean our country longed for us, as we for home?   545

CHORUS LEADER
So that I sighed, out of the darkness of my heart.

HERALD
Whence came this black thought to afflict the mind with fear?

CHORUS LEADER

Long since it was my silence kept disaster off.

HERALD

But how? There were some you feared when the kings went
away?

CHORUS LEADER

So much that as you said now, even death were grace.   550

HERALD

Well: the end has been good. And in the length of time
part of our fortune you could say held favorable,
but part we cursed again. And who, except the gods,
can live time through forever without any pain?
Were I to tell you of the hard work done, the nights   555
exposed, the cramped sea-quarters, the foul beds—what part
of day's disposal did we not cry out loud?
Ashore, the horror stayed with us and grew. We lay
against the ramparts of our enemies, and from
the sky, and from the ground, the meadow dews came out   560
to soak our clothes and fill our hair with lice. And if
I were to tell of wintertime, when all birds died,
the snows of Ida past endurance she sent down,
or summer heat, when in the lazy noon the sea
fell level and asleep under a windless sky—   565
but why live such grief over again? That time is gone
for us, and gone for those who died. Never again
need they rise up, nor care again for anything.
Why must a live man count the numbers of the slain,
why grieve at fortune's wrath that fades to break once more? 570
I call a long farewell to all our unhappiness.
For us, survivors of the Argive armament,
the pleasure wins, pain casts no weight in the opposite scale.
And here, in this sun's shining, we can boast aloud,
whose fame has gone with wings across the land and sea:°   575
"Upon a time the Argive host took Troy, and on

the houses of the gods who live in Hellas nailed
the spoils, to be the glory of days long ago."
And they who hear such things shall call this city bless'd
and the leaders of the host; and high the grace of god   580
shall be exalted, that did this. You have the story.

CHORUS LEADER
I must give way; your story shows that I was wrong.
Old men are always young enough to learn, with profit.
But Clytaemestra and her house must hear, above
others, this news that makes luxurious my life.   585

(Clytaemestra enters from the palace.)

CLYTAEMESTRA
I raised my cry of joy, and it was long ago
when the first beacon flare of message came by night
to speak of capture and of Ilium's overthrow.
But there was one who laughed at me, who said: "You trust   590
in beacons so, and you believe that Troy has fallen?
How like a woman, for the heart to lift so light."
Men spoke like that; they thought I wandered in my wits;
yet I made sacrifice, and in the womanish strain
voice after voice caught up the cry along the city   595
to echo in the temples of the gods and bless
and still the fragrant flame that melts the sacrifice.

Why should you tell me then the whole long tale at large
when from my lord himself I shall hear all the story?
But now, how best to speed my preparation to   600
receive my honored lord come home again—what else
is light more sweet for woman to behold than this,
to spread the gates before her husband home from war
and saved by god's hand?—take this message to the king:
Come, and with speed, back to the city that longs for him,   605
and may he find a wife within his house as true
as on the day he left her, watchdog of the house
gentle to him alone, fierce to his enemies,

and such a woman in all her ways as this, who has
not broken the seal upon her in the length of days.   610
With no man else have I known delight, nor any shame
of evil speech, more than I know how to temper bronze.

HERALD

A vaunt like this, so loaded as it is with truth,
it well becomes a highborn lady to proclaim.

CHORUS LEADER

Thus has she spoken to you, and well you understand,   615
words that impress interpreters whose thought is clear.
But tell me, herald; I would learn of Menelaus,
that power beloved in this land. Has he survived
also, and come with you back to his home again?

HERALD

I know no way to lie and make my tale so fair   620
that friends could reap joy of it for any length of time.

CHORUS LEADER

Is there no means to speak us fair, and yet tell the truth?
It will not hide, when truth and good are torn asunder.

HERALD

He is gone out of the sight of the Achaean host,
vessel and man alike. I speak no falsehood there.   625

CHORUS LEADER

Was it when he had put out from Ilium in your sight,
or did a storm that struck you both whirl him away?

HERALD

How like a master bowman you have hit the mark
and in your speech cut a long sorrow to brief stature.

CHORUS LEADER

But then the rumor in the host that sailed beside,   630
was it that he had perished, or might yet be living?

HERALD

No man knows. There is none could tell us that for sure
except the Sun, from whom this earth has life and increase.

CHORUS LEADER

How did this storm, by wrath of the divinities,
strike on our multitude at sea? How did it end? 635

HERALD

It is not well to stain the blessing of this day
with speech of evil weight. Such gods are honored apart.
And when the messenger of a shaken host, sad faced,
brings to his city news it prayed never to hear,
this scores one wound upon the body of the people; 640
and that from many houses many men are slain
by the two-lashed whip dear to the war god's hand, this turns
disaster double-bladed, bloodily made two.
The messenger so freighted with a charge of tears
should make his song of triumph at the Furies' door. 645
But, carrying the fair message of our hopes' salvation,
come home to a glad city's hospitality,
how shall I mix my gracious news with foul, and tell
of the storm on the Achaeans by god's anger sent?
For they, of old the deepest enemies, sea and fire, 650
made a conspiracy and gave their hand in oath
to blast in ruin our unhappy Argive army.
At night the sea began to rise in waves of death.
Ship against ship the Thracian stormwind shattered us,
and gored and split, our vessels, swept in violence 655
of storm and whirlwind, beaten by the breaking rain,
drove on in darkness, spun by the wicked shepherd's hand.
But when the sun came up again to light the dawn,
we saw the Aegean Sea blossoming with dead men,
the men of Achaea, and the wreckage of their ships. 660
For us, and for our ship, some god, no man, by guile
or by entreaty's force prevailing, laid his hand

upon the helm and brought us through with hull unscarred.
Life-giving fortune deigned to take our ship in charge
that neither riding in deep water she took the surf   665
nor drove to shoal and break upon some rocky shore.
But then, delivered from death at sea, in the pale day,
incredulous of our own luck, we shepherded
in our sad thoughts the fresh disaster of the fleet
so pitifully torn and shaken by the storm.   670
Now of these others, if there are any left alive
they speak of us as men who perished, must they not?
Even as we, who fear that they are gone. But may
it all come well in the end. For Menelaus: be sure
if any of them come back that he will be the first.   675
If he is still where some sun's gleam can track him down,
alive and open-eyed, by blessed hand of god
who willed that not yet should his seed be utterly gone,
there is some hope that he will still come home again.
You have heard all; and be sure, you have heard the truth.   680

(Exit the Herald to the side.)

CHORUS [*singing*]

STROPHE A

Who is he that named you so
fatally in every way?
Could it be some mind unseen
in divination of your destiny
shaping to the lips that name   685
for the bride of spears and blood,
Helen, a hell on earth? All too truly
hell for ships, hell for men and cities,
from the bower's soft curtained   690
and secluded luxury she sailed then,
driven on the giant west wind,
and armored men in their thousands came,
huntsmen down the oar blade's fading footprint   695

to struggle in blood with those
who by the banks of Simoeis
beached their hulls where the leaves break.

ANTISTROPHE A

And on Ilium in truth
in the likeness of the name   700
the sure purpose of the Wrath drove
marriage with death: for the guest board
shamed, and Zeus kindly to strangers,
the vengeance wrought on those men
who graced in too loud voice the bride-song   705
fallen to their lot to sing,
the kinsmen and the brothers.
And changing its song's measure
the ancient city of Priam   710
chants in high strain of lamentation,
calling Paris him of the fatal marriage;
for it endured its life's end
in desolation and tears
and the piteous blood of its people.   715

STROPHE B

Once a man fostered in his house
a lion cub, from the mother's milk
torn, craving the breast given.
In the first steps of its young life,   720
mild, it played with children
and delighted the old.
Caught in the arm's cradle
they pampered it like a newborn child,
shining-eyed and broken to the hand   725
to stay the stress of its hunger.

ANTISTROPHE B

But it grew with time, and the lion
in the blood strain came out; it repaid

thanks to those who had fostered it
in blood and death for the sheep flocks,   730
a grim feast forbidden.
The house reeked with blood run,
nor could its people beat down the bane,
the giant murderer's onslaught.
This thing they raised in their house was blessed   735
by god to be priest of destruction.

STROPHE C

And that which first came to the city of Ilium,
call it a dream of calm
and the wind dying,
the loveliness and luxury of much gold,   740
the melting shafts of the eyes' glances,
the blossom that breaks the heart with longing.
But she turned in midstep of her course to make
bitter the consummation,   745
whirling on Priam's people
to blight with her touch and nearness.
Zeus hospitable sent her,
a Vengeance to make brides weep.

ANTISTROPHE C

It was made long since, grown old now among men,   750
this saying: human wealth
grown to fullness of stature
breeds again nor dies without issue.
From high good fortune in the blood   755
blossoms the quenchless agony.
But far from others I hold my own
mind; only the act of evil
breeds others to follow,
young sins in its own likeness.   760
Houses clear in their right are given
children in all loveliness.

So Outrage aging is made ripe
in men's dark actions,
ripe with the young Outrage   765
late or soon, when the dawn of destiny
comes and birth is given
to the spirit none may fight nor beat down,
sinful Daring; and in those halls
the black-visaged Disasters stamped   770
in the likeness of their fathers.

But Righteousness still shines out
in the smoke of mean houses.
Her blessing is on the just man.   775
From high halls starred with gold by reeking hands
she turns back
with eyes that glance away to the simple in heart,
spurning the strength of gold
stamped false with flattery.   780
And all things she steers to fulfillment.

(*Enter Agamemnon from the side in a chariot,
with Cassandra beside him.*)

CHORUS [*chanting*]
Behold, my king: sacker of Troy's citadel,
own issue of Atreus.
How shall I hail you? How give honor   785
not shooting too high nor yet bending short
of this moment's fitness?
For many among men are they who set high
the show of honor, yet violate justice.
If one is distressed, all others are ready   790
to grieve with him: yet the teeth of sorrow
come nowhere near to their heart's edge.
And in joy likewise they show joy's semblance,
and torture the face to the false smile.

Yet the good shepherd, who knows his flock,   795
the eyes of men cannot lie to him,
who with water of feigned
love seem to smile from the true heart.
But I: when you marshaled this armament
for Helen's sake, I will not hide it,   800
in ugly style you were written in my heart
for steering aslant the mind's course
to bring home by blood
sacrifice and dead men that wild spirit.°
But now, in love drawn up from the deep heart,   805
not skimmed at the edge, we hail you.
You have won; your labor is made gladness.
Ask everyone: you will learn in time
which of your citizens have been just
in the city's service, which were reckless.   810

AGAMEMNON

To Argos first, and to the gods within the land,
I must give due greeting; they have worked with me to bring
me home; they helped me in the vengeance I have wrought
on Priam's city. Not from the lips of men the gods
heard justice, but in one firm cast they laid their votes   815
within the urn of blood that Ilium must die
and all her people; while above the opposite vase
the hand hovered and there was hope, but no vote fell.
The storm clouds of their ruin live; the ash that dies
upon them gushes still in smoke their pride of wealth.   820
For all this we must thank the gods with grace of much
high praise and memory, we who fenced within our toils
of wrath the city; and, because one woman strayed,
the beast of Argos broke them, the fierce young within
the horse, the armored people who marked out their leap   825
against the setting of the Pleiades. A wild
and bloody lion swarmed above the towers of Troy
to glut its hunger lapping at the blood of kings.

This to the gods, a prelude strung to length of words.
But, for the thought you spoke, I heard and I remember   830
and stand beside you. For I say that it is true.
In few men is it part of nature to respect
a friend's prosperity without begrudging him,
as envy's wicked poison settling to the heart
piles up the pain in one sick with unhappiness,   835
who, staggered under sufferings that are all his own,
winces again to the vision of a neighbor's bliss.
And I can speak, for I have seen, I know it well,
this mirror of companionship, this shadow's ghost,
all those who seemed my friends in their sincerity.   840
Just one of them, Odysseus, he who sailed unwilling,
once yoked to me pulled all his weight, nor ever slacked.
Dead though he be or living, I can say it still.

Now in the business of the city and the gods
we must ordain full conclave of all citizens   845
and take our counsel. We shall see what element
is strong, and plan that it shall keep its virtue still.
But that which must be healed—we shall use medicine,
or burn, or amputate, with kind intention, take
all means at hand that might beat down corruption's pain.   850
So to the king's house and the home about the hearth
I take my way, with greeting to the gods within
who sent me forth, and who have brought me home once
     more.
My prize was conquest; may it never fail again.

CLYTAEMESTRA
Grave gentlemen of Argolis assembled here,   855
I take no shame to speak aloud before you all
the love I bear my husband. In the lapse of time
modesty fades; it is human.
                                          What I tell you now
I learned not from another; this was my own sad life
all the long years this man was gone at Ilium.   860

It is evil and a thing of terror when a wife
sits in the house forlorn with no man by, and hears
rumors that like a fever die to break again,
and men come in with news of fear, and on their heels
another messenger, with worse news to cry aloud   865
here in this house. Had Agamemnon taken all
the wounds of which the tale was carried home to me,
he had been cut full of gashes like a fishing net.
If he had died each time that rumor told his death,
he must have been some triple-bodied Geryon   870
back from the dead with threefold cloak of earth upon
his body, and killed once for every shape assumed.
Because such tales broke out forever on my rest,
many a time they cut me down and freed my throat   875
from the noose overslung where I had caught it fast.
And therefore is your son, in whom my love and yours
are sealed and pledged, not here to stand with us today,
Orestes. It were right; yet do not be amazed.
Strophius of Phocis, comrade in arms and faithful friend   880
to you, is keeping him. He spoke to me of peril
on two counts; of your danger under Ilium,
and here, of revolution and the clamorous people
who might cast down the council—since it lies in men's
nature to trample on the fighter already down.   885
Such my excuse to you, and without subterfuge.

For me: the rippling springs that were my tears have dried
utterly up, nor left one drop within. I keep
the pain upon my eyes where late at night I wept
over the beacons long ago set for your sake,   890
untended left forever. In the midst of dreams
the whisper that a gnat's thin wings could winnow broke
my sleep apart. I thought I saw you suffer wounds
more than the time that slept with me could ever hold.

Now all my suffering is past; with griefless heart   895
I hail this man, the watchdog of the fold and hall;

the rope that keeps the ship afloat; the post to grip
groundward the towering roof; a father's single child;
land seen by sailors after all their hope was gone;
splendor of daybreak shining from the night of storm;   900
the running spring a parched wayfarer strays upon.
Oh, it is sweet to escape from all necessity!

Such is my greeting to him, that he well deserves.
Let none bear malice; for the harm that went before
I took, and it was great.
                    Now, my beloved one,   905
step from your chariot; yet let not your foot, my lord,
sacker of Ilium, touch the earth. My maidens there!
Why this delay? Your task has been appointed you,
to strew the ground before his feet with tapestries.
Let there spring up into the house he never hoped   910
to see, where Justice leads him in, a crimson path.

In all things else, my heart's unsleeping care shall act
with the gods' aid to set aright what fate ordained.

        (Clytaemestra's handmaidens spread a red
          carpet between the chariot and the door.)

AGAMEMNON

Daughter of Leda, you who kept my house for me,
there is one way your welcome matched my absence well.   915
You strained it to great length. Yet properly to praise
me thus belongs by right to other lips, not yours.
And all this—do not try in woman's ways to make
me delicate, nor, as if I were some Asian prince
bow down to earth and with wide mouth cry out to me,   920
nor cross my path with jealousy by strewing the ground
with robes. Such state befits the gods, and none beside.
I am a mortal, a man; I cannot trample upon
these tinted splendors without fear thrown in my path.
I tell you, as a man, not god, to reverence me.   925

Discordant is the murmur at such treading down
of lovely things; while god's most lordly gift to man
is decency of mind. Call that man only bless'd
who has in sweet tranquility brought his life to close.
If I could only act as such, my hope is good. 930

CLYTAEMESTRA
Yet tell me this one thing, and do not cross my will.

AGAMEMNON
My will is mine. I shall not make it soft for you.

CLYTAEMESTRA
Might you in fear have vowed to do such things for god?

AGAMEMNON
Only if the one who advised so knew the full purpose.°

CLYTAEMESTRA
If Priam had won as you have, what would he have done? 935

AGAMEMNON
I well believe he might have walked on tapestries.

CLYTAEMESTRA
Be not ashamed before the criticism of men.

AGAMEMNON
The people murmur, and their voice is great in strength.

CLYTAEMESTRA
Yet he who goes unenvied shall not be admired.

AGAMEMNON
Surely this lust for conflict is not womanlike? 940

CLYTAEMESTRA
Yet for the mighty even to give way is grace.

AGAMEMNON
Does such a victory as this mean so much to you?

CLYTAEMESTRA

Oh yield! The power is yours. Freely give way to me.

AGAMEMNON

Since you must have it—here, let someone with all speed
take off these sandals, slaves for my feet to tread upon.   945
And as I crush these garments stained from the rich sea
let no god's eyes of hatred strike me from afar.
Great the extravagance, and great the shame I feel
to spoil such treasure and such silver's worth of weaving.

So much for all this. Take this stranger girl within   950
now, and be kind. The conqueror who uses softly
his power is watched benevolently by god from afar,
and this slave's yoke is one no man will wear from choice.
Gift of the host to me, and flower exquisite
from all my many treasures, she attends me here.   955

Now since my will was bent to listen to you in this
my feet crush crimson as I pass within the hall.

CLYTAEMESTRA

The sea is there, and who shall drain its yield? It breeds
precious as silver, ever of itself renewed,
the purple ooze wherein our garments shall be dipped.   960
And by god's grace this house keeps full sufficiency
of all. Poverty is a thing beyond its thought.
I could have vowed to trample many splendors down
had such decree been ordained from the oracles
those days when all my study was to bring home your life.   965
For when the root lives yet the leaves will come again
to fence the house with shade against the Dog Star's heat,
and now you have come home to keep your hearth and
    house,
you bring with you the symbol of our winter's warmth;
and when Zeus ripens the green clusters into wine   970
there shall be coolness in the house upon those days
because the master ranges his own halls once more.

Zeus, Zeus accomplisher, accomplish these my prayers.
Let your mind bring these things to pass. It is your will.

(Agamemnon and Clytaemestra enter the palace.
Cassandra remains in the chariot.)

CHORUS [*singing*]

STROPHE A

Why must this persistent fear   975
beat its wings so ceaselessly
and so close against my mantic heart?
Why this strain unwanted, unrepaid, thus prophetic?
Nor can valor of good hope   980
seated near the chambered depth
of the spirit cast it out
as dreams of dark fancy; and yet time
has buried in the mounding sand
the sea cables since that day°   985
when against Ilium
the army and the ships put to sea.

ANTISTROPHE A

Yet I have seen with these eyes,
Agamemnon home again.
Still the spirit sings, drawing deep   990
from within this unlyric threnody of the Fury.
Hope is gone utterly;
the sweet strength is far away.
Surely this is not fantasy.   995
Surely it is real, this whirl of drifts
that spin the stricken heart.
Still I pray; may all this
expectation fade as vanity
into unfulfillment, and not be.   1000

STROPHE B

Yet it is true: the high strength of men
knows no content with limitation. Sickness

chambered beside it beats at the wall between.
Man's fate that sets a true   1005
course yet may strike upon
the blind and sudden reefs of disaster.°
But if before such time, fear
throw overboard some precious thing
of the cargo, with deliberate cast,   1010
not all the house, laboring
with weight of ruin, shall go down,
nor sink the hull deep within the sea.
And great and affluent the gift of Zeus
in yield of plowed acres year on year   1015
makes void again sick starvation.

ANTISTROPHE B
But when the black and mortal blood of man
has fallen to the ground before his feet, who then   1020
can sing spells to call it back again?
Did Zeus not warn us once
when he struck to impotence
Asclepius, who in truth charmed back the dead men?
Had the gods not so ordained   1025
that fate should stand against fate
to check any man's excess,
my heart now would have outrun speech
to break forth the water of its grief.
But this is so; I murmur deep in darkness   1030
sore at heart; my hope is gone now
ever again to unwind some crucial good
from the flames about my heart.

(Enter Clytaemestra from the palace.)

CLYTAEMESTRA
Cassandra, you may go within the house as well,   1035
since Zeus in no unkindness has ordained that you
must share our lustral water, stand with the great throng

of slaves that flock to the altar of our household god.
Step from this chariot, then, and do not be so proud.
And think—they say that long ago Alcmene's son   1040
was sold in bondage and endured the bread of slaves.
But if constraint of fact forces you to such fate,
be glad indeed for masters ancient in their wealth.
They who have reaped success beyond their dreams of hope
are savage above need and standard toward their slaves.   1045
From us you shall have all you have the right to ask.

CHORUS LEADER

What she has spoken is for you, and clear enough.
Fenced in these fatal nets wherein you find yourself
you should obey her if you can; perhaps you cannot.

CLYTAEMESTRA

Unless she uses speech incomprehensible,   1050
barbarian, wild as the swallow's song, I speak
within her understanding, and she must obey.

CHORUS LEADER

Go with her. What she bids is best in circumstance
that binds you now. Obey, and leave this chariot seat.

CLYTAEMESTRA

I have no leisure to stand outside the house and waste   1055
time on this woman. At the central altarstone
the flocks are standing, ready for the sacrifice
we make to this glad day we never hoped to see.
You: if you are obeying my commands at all, be quick.
But if in ignorance you fail to comprehend,   1060
speak not, but make with your barbarian hand some sign.

CHORUS LEADER

I think this stranger girl needs some interpreter
who understands. She is like some captive animal.

CLYTAEMESTRA

No, she is in the passion of her own wild thoughts.

Leaving her captured city she has come to us   1065
untrained to take the curb, and will not understand
until her rage and strength have foamed away in blood.
I shall throw down no more commands for her contempt.

(Exit Clytaemestra into the palace.)

CHORUS LEADER
I, though, shall not be angry, for I pity her.
Come down, poor creature, leave the empty car. Give way   1070
to compulsion and take up the yoke that shall be yours.

(Cassandra steps down from the chariot.)

CASSANDRA [*singing throughout the following interchange, while the
Chorus Leader speaks in response*]
  Oh shame upon the earth!
  Apollo, Apollo!

CHORUS LEADER
You cry on Loxias in agony? He is not
the one who usually has to do with grief.   1075

CASSANDRA
  Oh shame upon the earth!
  Apollo, Apollo!

CHORUS LEADER
Now once again in bitter voice she calls upon
this god, who has not part in any lamentation.

CASSANDRA
  Apollo, Apollo!   1080
  Lord of the ways, my ruin.
  You have undone me once again, and utterly.

CHORUS LEADER
I think she will be prophetic of her own disaster.
Even in the slave's heart the gift divine lives on.

CASSANDRA
  Apollo, Apollo!   1085

Lord of the ways, my ruin.
Where have you led me now at last? What house is this?

CHORUS LEADER

The house of the Atreidae. If you understand
not that, I can tell you; and so much at least is true.

CASSANDRA

No, but a house that god hates, guilty within   1090
of kindred blood shed, torture of its own,°
the shambles for men's butchery, the dripping floor.

CHORUS LEADER

The stranger is keen-scented like some hound upon
the trail of blood that leads her to discovered death.

CASSANDRA

Behold there the witnesses to my faith.   1095
The small children wail for their own death
and the flesh roasted that their father fed upon.

CHORUS LEADER

We had been told before of this prophetic fame
of yours: we want no prophets in this place at all.

CASSANDRA

Ah, for shame, what can she purpose now?   1100
What is this new and huge
stroke of atrocity she plans within the house
to beat down the beloved beyond hope of healing?
Rescue is far away.

CHORUS LEADER

I can make nothing of these prophecies. The rest   1105
I understood; the city is full of the sound of them.

CASSANDRA

So cruel then, that you can do this thing?
The husband of your own bed
to bathe bright with water—how shall I speak the end?

This thing shall be done with speed. The hand gropes now, and the
  other   1110
hand follows in turn.

CHORUS LEADER

No, I am lost. After the darkness of her speech
I go bewildered in a mist of prophecies.

CASSANDRA

No, no, see there! What is that thing that shows?
Is it some net of death?   1115
Or is the trap the woman there, the murderess?
Let now the slakeless fury in the race
rear up to howl aloud over this monstrous death.

CHORUS LEADER

Upon what demon in the house do you call, to raise
the cry of triumph? All your speech makes dark my hope.   1120

CHORUS [*singing now and throughout the following interchange with*
Cassandra, who continues to sing as well]
And to the heart below trickles the pale drop
as in the hour of death
timed to our sunset and the mortal radiance.
Ruin is near, and swift.

CASSANDRA

See there, see there! Keep from his mate the bull.   1125
Caught in the folded web's
entanglement she pinions him and with the black horn
strikes. And he crumples in the watered bath.
Guile, I tell you, and death there in the caldron wrought.

CHORUS LEADER

I am not proud in skill to guess at prophecies,   1130
yet even I can see the evil in this thing.

CHORUS

From divination what good ever has come to men?
Art, and multiplication of words

drifting through tangled evil bring
terror to them that hear.   1135

CASSANDRA

Alas, alas for the wretchedness of my ill-starred life.
This pain flooding the song of sorrow is mine alone.
Why have you brought me here in all unhappiness?
Why, why? Except to die with him? What else could be?

CHORUS

You are possessed of god, inspired at heart   1140
to sing your own death
song, the wild lyric as
in clamor for Itys, Itys over and over again
her long life of tears weeping forever grieves
the brown nightingale.   1145

CASSANDRA

Oh for the nightingale's pure song and a fate like hers.
With fashion of beating wings the gods clothed her about
and a sweet life they gave her and without lamentation.
But mine is the sheer edge of the tearing iron.

CHORUS

Whence come, beat upon beat, driven of god,   1150
vain passions of tears?
Whence your cries, terrified, clashing in horror,
in wrought melody and the singing speech?
Whence take you the marks to this path of prophecy
and speech of terror?   1155

CASSANDRA

Oh marriage of Paris, death to the men beloved!
Alas, Scamandrus, water my fathers drank.
There was a time I too at your springs
drank and grew strong. Ah me,
for now beside the deadly rivers, Cocytus   1160
and Acheron, I must cry out my prophecies.

CHORUS

What is this word, too clear, you have uttered now?
A child could understand.
And deep within goes the stroke of the dripping fang
as mortal pain at the trebled song of your agony 1165
shivers the heart to hear.

CASSANDRA

O sorrow, sorrow of my city dragged to uttermost death.
O sacrifices my father made at the wall.
Flocks of the pastured sheep slaughtered there.
And no use at all 1170
to save our city from its pain inflicted now.
And I too, with brain ablaze in fever, shall go down.

CHORUS

This follows the run of your song.
Is it, in cruel force of weight,
some divinity kneeling upon you brings 1175
the death song of your passionate suffering?
I cannot see the end.

CASSANDRA [*now speaking*]

No longer shall my prophecies like some young girl
new-married glance from under veils, but bright and strong
as winds blow into morning and the sun's uprise 1180
shall wax along the swell like some great wave, to burst
at last upon the shining of this agony.
Now I will tell you plainly and from no cryptic speech;
bear me then witness, running at my heels upon
the scent of these old brutal things done long ago. 1185
There is a choir that sings as one, that shall not again
leave this house ever; the song thereof breaks harsh with
    menace.
And drugged to double fury on the wine of men's
blood shed, there lurks forever here a drunken rout
of ingrown vengeful spirits never to be cast forth. 1190

Hanging above the hall they chant their song of hate
and the old sin, and taking up the strain in turn
spit curses on that man who spoiled his brother's bed.
Did I go wide, or hit, like a real archer? Am I
some swindling seer who hawks his lies from door to door?   1195
Upon your oath, bear witness that I know by heart
the legend of ancient wickedness within this house.

CHORUS LEADER [*speaking*]
And how could an oath, though cast in rigid honesty,
do any good? And still we stand amazed at you,
reared in an alien city far beyond the sea;   1200
how can you strike, as if you had been there, the truth?

CASSANDRA
Apollo was the seer who set me to this work.

CHORUS LEADER
Struck with some passion for you, and himself a god?

CASSANDRA
There was a time I blushed to speak about these things.

CHORUS LEADER
True; they who prosper take on airs more delicate.   1205

CASSANDRA
Yes, then; he wrestled with me, and he breathed delight.

CHORUS LEADER
Did you come to the getting of children then, the two of you?

CASSANDRA
I promised that to Loxias, but I broke my word.

CHORUS LEADER
Were you already possessed with the skills of god?

CASSANDRA
Yes; even then I read my city's destinies.   1210

CHORUS LEADER

So Loxias' wrath did you no harm? How could that be?

CASSANDRA

For this my trespass, none believed me ever again.

CHORUS LEADER

But we do; all that you foretell seems true to us.

CASSANDRA

But this is evil, see!
Now once again the pain of grim, true prophecy   1215
shivers my whirling brain in a storm of things foreseen.
Look there, see what is hovering above the house,
so small and young, imaged as in the shadow of dreams,
like children almost, killed by those most dear to them,
and their hands filled with their own flesh, as food to eat.   1220
I see them holding out the inward parts, the vitals,
oh pitiful, that meat their father tasted of . . .
I tell you: There is one that plots vengeance for this,
the strengthless lion rolling in his master's bed,
who keeps, ah me, the house against his lord's return;   1225
my lord too, now that I wear the slave's yoke on my neck.
King of the ships, who tore up Ilium by the roots,
what does he know of this accursed bitch, who licks
his hand, who fawns on him with lifted ears, who like
a secret death shall strike the coward's stroke, nor fail?   1230
No, this is daring when the female shall strike down
the male. What can I call her and be right? What beast
of loathing? Viper double-fanged, or Scylla witch
holed in the rocks and bane of men that range the sea;
smoldering mother of death to breathe relentless hate   1235
on those most dear. How she stood up and howled aloud
and unashamed, as at the breaking point of battle,
in feigned gladness for his salvation from the sea!
What does it matter now if men believe or no?
What is to come will come. And soon you too will stand   1240
beside, to murmur in pity that my words were true.

CHORUS LEADER

Thyestes' feast upon the flesh of his own children
I understand in terror at the thought, and fear
is on me hearing truth and no tale fabricated.
The rest: I heard it, but wander still far from the course.   1245

CASSANDRA

I tell you, you shall look on Agamemnon dead.

CHORUS LEADER

Peace, peace, poor woman; put those bitter lips to sleep.

CASSANDRA

Useless; there is no god of healing in this story.

CHORUS LEADER

Not if it must be; may it somehow fail to come.

CASSANDRA

You pray, yes; but they—they plan to strike, and kill.   1250

CHORUS LEADER

What man is it who moves this beastly thing to be?

CASSANDRA

What man? You did mistake my divination then.

CHORUS LEADER

It may be; I could not follow through the schemer's plan.

CASSANDRA

Yet I know Greek; I think I know it far too well.

CHORUS LEADER

And Pythian oracles are Greek, yet hard to read.   1255

CASSANDRA

Oh, flame and pain that sweeps me once again! My lord,
Apollo, King of Light, the pain, aye me, the pain!
This is the woman-lioness, who goes to bed
with the wolf, when her proud lion ranges far away,

and she will cut me down; as a wife mixing drugs   1260
she wills to shred the virtue of my punishment
into her bowl of wrath as she makes sharp the blade
against her man, death that he brought a mistress home.
Why do I wear these mockeries upon my body,
this staff of prophecy, these garlands at my throat?   1265
At least I will spoil you before I die. Out, down,
break, damn you! This for all that you have done to me.
Make someone else, not me, luxurious in disaster . . .
Lo now, this is Apollo who has stripped me here
of my prophetic robes. He watched me all the time   1270
wearing this glory, mocked by all, my dearest ones
who hated me with all their hearts, so vain, so wrong;
called like some gypsy wandering from door to door
beggar, corrupt, half-starved, and I endured it all.
And now the seer has done with me, his prophetess,   1275
and led me into such a place as this, to die.
Lost are my father's altars, but the block is here
to reek with sacrificial blood, my own. We two
must die, yet die not vengeless by the gods. For there
shall come one to avenge us also, born to slay   1280
his mother, and to wreak death for his father's blood.
Outlaw and wanderer, driven far from his own land,
he will come back to cope these stones of inward hate.
For this is a strong oath and sworn by the high gods,°
that he shall cast them headlong for his father felled.   1285
Why am I then so pitiful? Why must I weep?
Since once I saw the citadel of Ilium
die as it died, and those who broke the city, doomed
by the gods, fare as they have fared accordingly,
I will go through with it. I too will take my fate.   1290
I call as on the gates of death upon these gates
to pray only for this thing, that the stroke be true,
and that with no convulsion, with a rush of blood
in painless death, I may close up these eyes, and rest.

CHORUS LEADER

O woman much enduring and so greatly wise,   1295
you have said much. But if this thing you know be true,
this death that comes upon you, how can you, serene,
walk to the altar like a driven ox of god?

CASSANDRA

Friends, there is no escape for any longer time.

CHORUS LEADER

Yet the last bit of time is to be honored most.   1300

CASSANDRA

The day is here and now; I cannot win by flight.

CHORUS LEADER

Woman, be sure your heart is brave; you can endure much.

CASSANDRA

None but the most unhappy ever hear such praise.

CHORUS LEADER

Yet there is a grace on mortals who so nobly die.

CASSANDRA

Alas for you, father, and for your lordly sons.   1305
Ah!

CHORUS LEADER

What now? What terror whirls you backward from the door?

CASSANDRA

Foul, foul!

CHORUS LEADER

What foulness then, unless some horror in the mind?

CASSANDRA

That room within reeks with blood like a slaughterhouse.

CHORUS LEADER

What then? Only these animals butchered at the hearth.   1310

CASSANDRA

There is a breath about it like an open grave.

CHORUS LEADER

This is no Syrian pride of frankincense you mean.

CASSANDRA

So. I am going in, and mourning as I go
my death and Agamemnon's. Let my life be done.
Ah friends,   1315
truly this is no wild bird fluttering at a bush,
nor vain my speech. Bear witness to me when I die,
when falls for me, a woman slain, another woman,
and when a man dies for this wickedly mated man.
Here in my death I claim this stranger's grace of you.   1320

CHORUS LEADER

Poor wretch, I pity you the fate you see so clear.

CASSANDRA

Yet once more will I speak, and not this time my own
death's threnody. I call upon the Sun in prayer
against that ultimate shining when the avengers strike
these monsters down in blood, that they avenge as well   1325
one simple slave who died, a small thing, lightly killed.
Alas, poor men, their destiny. When all goes well
a shadow will overthrow it. If it be unkind
one stroke of a wet sponge wipes all the picture out;
and that is far the most unhappy thing of all.   1330

(Exit Cassandra into the palace.)

CHORUS [chanting]

High fortune is a thing insatiable
for mortals. There is no man who shall point
his finger to drive it back from the door
and speak the words: "Come no longer."
Now to this man the blessed ones have given   1335
Priam's city to be captured

and return in the gods' honor.
Must he give blood for generations gone,
die for those slain and in death pile up
more death to come for the blood shed?   1340
What mortal else who hears shall claim
he was born immune to the demon of harm?

AGAMEMNON   *(Inside the house.)*
  Ah, I am struck a deadly blow and deep within!

CHORUS LEADER
  Silence: who cried out that he was stabbed to death within
    the house?

AGAMEMNON
  Ah me, again, they struck again. I am wounded twice.   1345

CHORUS LEADER
  How the king cried out aloud to us! I believe the thing is
    done.
  Come, let us put our heads together, try to find some safe way
    out.

CHORUS   *(Each member speaking excitedly in turn.)*
  Listen, let me tell you what I think is best to do.
  Let the herald call all citizens to rally here.

  No, better to burst in upon them now, at once,   1350
  and take them with the blood still running from their blades.

  I am with this man and I cast my vote to him.
  Act now. This is the perilous and instant time.

  Anyone can see it, by these first steps they have taken,
  they purpose to be tyrants here upon our city.   1355

  Yes, for we waste time, while they trample to the ground
  deliberation's honor, and their hands sleep not.

  I cannot tell which counsel of yours to call my own.
  It is the man of action who can plan as well.°

I feel as he does; nor can I see how by words   1360
we shall set the dead man back upon his feet again.

Do you mean, to drag our lives out long, that we must yield
to those shaming the house, and leadership of such as these?

No, we can never endure that; better to be killed.
Death is a softer thing by far than tyranny.   1365

Shall we, by no more proof than that he cried in pain,
be sure, as by divination, that our lord is dead?

Yes, we should know what is true before we speak our mind.
Here is sheer guessing and far different from sure
    knowledge.

From all sides the voices multiply to make me choose   1370
this course; to learn first how it stands with Agamemnon.

*(The doors of the palace open, disclosing the bodies of Agamemnon
and Cassandra, with Clytaemestra standing over them.)*

CLYTAEMESTRA
    Much have I said before to serve necessity,
    but I will feel no shame now to unsay it all.
    How else could I, arming hate against hateful men
    disguised in seeming tenderness, fence high the nets   1375
    of ruin beyond overleaping? Thus to me
    the conflict born of ancient bitterness is not
    a thing new thought upon, but pondered deep in time.
    I stand now where I struck him down. The thing is done.
    Thus have I wrought, and I will not deny it now.   1380
    That he might not escape nor beat aside his death,
    as fishermen cast their huge circling nets, I spread
    deadly abundance of rich robes, and caught him fast.
    I struck him twice. In two great cries of agony
    he buckled at the knees and fell. When he was down   1385
    I struck him the third blow, in thanks and reverence
    to Zeus beneath the ground, the prayed-for Savior of the dead.
    Thus he went down, and the life struggled out of him;

and as he died he spattered me with the dark red
and violent driven rain of bitter-savored blood   1390
to make me glad, as plants stand strong amidst the showers
of god in glory at the birthtime of the buds.

These being the facts, elders of Argos assembled here,
be glad, if it be your pleasure; but for me, I glory.
If libations were proper to pour above the slain,   1395
this man deserved, more than deserved, such sacrament.
He filled our cup with evil things unspeakable
and now himself come home has drunk it to the dregs.

CHORUS LEADER

We stand here stunned. How can you speak this way, with
    mouth
so arrogant, to vaunt above your fallen lord?   1400

CLYTAEMESTRA

You try me out as if I were a woman and vain;
but my heart is not fluttered as I speak before you.
You know it. You can praise or blame me as you wish;
it is all one to me. That man is Agamemnon,
my husband; he is dead; the work of this right hand   1405
that struck in strength of righteousness. And that is that.

CHORUS [singing]

STROPHE A

Woman, what evil thing planted upon the earth
or dragged from the running salt sea could you have tasted now
to show such brutality and walk in the people's hate?
You have cast away, you have cut away. You shall go homeless now, 1410
crushed with men's bitterness.

CLYTAEMESTRA

Now it is I you vote to be cast out from my city
with men's hate heaped and curses roaring in my ears.
Yet look upon this dead man; you did not cross him once
when with no thought more than as if a beast were
    butchered,   1415

when his ranged pastures swarmed with the deep fleece of
  flocks,
he slaughtered at the altar his own child, my pain
grown into love, to charm away the winds of Thrace.
Were you not bound to hunt him then clear of this soil
for the guilt stained upon him? Yet you hear what I   1420
have done, and lo, you are a stern judge. But I say to you:
go on and threaten me, but know that I am ready,
if fairly you can beat me down beneath your hand,
for you to rule; but if the god grant otherwise,
you shall be taught—too late, for sure—to keep your place.   1425

CHORUS [singing]

ANTISTROPHE A

Big are your thoughts, your speech is a clamor of pride.
Swung to the red act drives the fury within your brain
signed clear in the flecks of blood on your eyes.
Yet to come is stroke given for stroke
avenging, when you are forlorn of friends.   1430

CLYTAEMESTRA

Now hear you this, the right behind my sacrament:
By my child's Justice driven to fulfillment, by
her Wrath and Fury, to whom I sacrificed this man,
the hope that walks my chambers is not traced with fear
while yet Aegisthus makes the fire shine in my hearth,   1435
my good friend, now as always, who shall be for us
the shield of our defiance, no weak thing; while he,
this other, is fallen, stained with this woman you behold,
plaything of all the golden girls at Ilium;
and here lies she, the captive of his spear, who saw   1440
wonders, who shared his bed, the wise in revelations
and loving mistress, who yet knew the feel as well
of the men's rowing benches. Their reward is not
unworthy. He lies there; and she who swanlike cried
aloud her lyric dying lamentation, now   1445

lies next to him, his lover, and to me has given
a delicate excitement, spicing my delight.°

CHORUS [*singing*]

O that in speed, without pain
and the slow bed of sickness,
death could come to us now, death that forever   1450
carries sleep without ending, now that our lord is down,
our shield, kindest of men,
who for a woman's grace suffered so much,
struck down at last by a woman.

[*chanting*]
Alas, Helen, crazed heart   1455
for the multitudes, for the thousand lives
you killed under Troy's shadow:
now as your final memorial,
you're adorned in blood never to be washed out.   1460
Surely a demon then
of Strife walked in the house, men's agony.

CLYTAEMESTRA [*chanting throughout the following interchange*
with the Chorus]

No, be not so harsh, and don't invoke
in prayer death's ending,
neither turn all wrath against Helen
for men dead, that she alone killed   1465
all those Danaan lives, to work
the grief that is past all healing.

CHORUS [*singing*]

ANTISTROPHE B

Spirit that kneels on this house and on the two
strains of the blood of Tantalus,
in the hands and hearts of women you steer   1470
the strength tearing my heart.
Standing above the corpse, obscene

as some carrion crow it sings
the crippled song and is proud.°

CLYTAEMESTRA

Now have you set the speech of your lips   1475
straight, calling by name
the spirit thrice glutted that lives in this race.
From it, deep in the nerve is given
the love and the blood drunk, that before
the old wound dries, it bleeds again.   1480

CHORUS [singing]

STROPHE C

Surely it is a huge
and angry spirit haunting the house you cry;
alas, the bitter story
of a doom that shall never be done with;
and all through Zeus, Zeus,   1485
first cause, prime mover.
For what thing without Zeus is done among mortals?
What here is without god's blessing?

[chanting]
O king, my king,
how shall I weep for you?   1490
What can I say out of my heart of pity?
Caught in this spider's web you lie.
Your life gasped out in indecent death,
struck prone to this shameful bed
by your lady's hand of treachery   1495
and the stroke twin-edged of the iron.

CLYTAEMESTRA

Can you claim I have done this?
Speak of me never
more as the wife of Agamemnon.°
In the image of this corpse's queen   1500

the old stark avenger
of Atreus for his revel of hate
struck down this man,
last blood for the slaughtered children.

CHORUS [*singing*]

What man shall testify   1505
your hands are clean of this murder?
How? How? Yet from his father's blood
might swarm some fiend to assist you.
The black ruin that shoulders
through the streaming blood of brothers   1510
strides at last where he shall win requital
for the children who were eaten.

[*chanting*]
O king, my king
how shall I weep for you?
What can I say out of my heart of pity?   1515
Caught in this spider's web you lie,
your life gasped out in indecent death,
struck prone to this shameful bed
by your lady's hand of treachery
and the stroke twin-edged of the iron.   1520

CLYTAEMESTRA

No shame, I think, in the death given
this man. And did he not
first of all in this house wreak death
by treachery?
The flower of this man's love and mine,   1525
Iphigeneia of the many tears—
he dealt with her even as he has suffered now.°
So let his speech in Death's house be not loud.
With the sword he struck;
with the sword he paid for his own act.

CHORUS [*singing*]

My thoughts are swept away and I go bewildered.   1530
Where shall I turn the brain's
activity in speed when the house is falling?
There is fear in the beat of the blood rain breaking
wall and tower. The drops come thicker.
Still fate grinds on yet more stones the blade   1535
for more acts of terror.

[*chanting*]
Earth, my earth, why did you not fold me under
before ever I saw this man lie dead
fenced in by the tub of silver?   1540
Who shall bury him? Who shall mourn him?
Shall you dare this who have killed
your lord? Make lamentation,
render the graceless grace to his soul
for huge things done in wickedness?   1545
Who over this great man's grave shall lay
the blessing of tears
worked soberly from a true heart?   1550

CLYTAEMESTRA

Not for you to speak of such tendance.
Through us he fell,
by us he died; we shall bury.
There will be no tears in this house for him.
It must be Iphigeneia   1555
his child—who else
shall greet her father by the whirling stream
and the ferry of tears
to close him in her arms and kiss him.

CHORUS [*singing*]

Here is anger for anger. Between them   1560
who shall judge lightly?

The spoiler is robbed; he killed, he has paid.
The truth stands ever beside god's throne
eternal: he who has done shall suffer; that is law.
Then who shall tear the curse from their blood?   1565
The house is glued to ruin.

CLYTAEMESTRA

You see truth in the future
at last. Yet I wish
to seal my oath with the Spirit
in the house: I will endure all things as they stand   1570
now, hard though it be. Hereafter
let it go forth to make bleed with death
and guilt the houses of others.
I will take some small
measure of our riches, and be content
that I swept from these halls   1575
the murder, the sin, and the fury.

(Enter Aegisthus from the side, with his armed bodyguard.)

AEGISTHUS

O splendor and triumph of this day of justice!
Now I can say once more that the high gods look down
on mortal crimes to vindicate the right at last,
now that I see this man—sweet sight—before me here   1580
sprawled in the tangling nets of fury, to atone
the calculated evil of his father's hand.
For Atreus, this man's father, King of Argolis—
I tell you the clear story—drove my father forth,
Thyestes, his own brother, who had challenged him   1585
in his king's right—forth from his city and his home.
Yet poor Thyestes came again to supplicate
the hearth, and win some grace. He found a safe portion
nor soiled the doorstone of his fathers with blood spilled.
Not his own blood. But Atreus, this man's godless sire,   1590
angrily hospitable set a feast for him,
in seeming a glad day of fresh meat slain and good

cheer; then served my father his own children's flesh
to feed on. For he carved away the extremities,
hands, feet, and cut the flesh apart, and covered them   1595
served in a dish to my father at his table apart,
who with no thought for the featureless meal before him ate
that ghastly food whose curse works now before your eyes.
But when he knew the terrible thing that he had done,
he spat the dead meat from him with a cry, recoiled   1600
and kicked the table over, pledging with strength his curse:
"Thus crash in ruin all the seed of Pleisthenes."
Out of such acts you see this dead man stricken here,
and it was I, in my right, who wrought this murder, I
third-born to my unhappy father, and with him   1605
driven, a helpless baby in arms, to banishment.
Yet I grew up, and justice brought me home again,
till from afar I laid my hands upon this man,
since it was I who pieced together the deadly plot.
Now I can die in honor again, if die I must,   1610
having seen him caught in the nets of his just punishment.

CHORUS LEADER
Aegisthus, this strong vaunting in distress is vile.
You claim that you deliberately killed the king,
you, and you only, planned the pity of this death.
I tell you then: There shall be no escape, your head   1615
shall face the stones of anger from the people's hands.

AEGISTHUS
So loud from you, stooped to the meanest rowing bench
with the ship's masters lordly on the deck above?
You are old men; well, you shall learn how hard it is,
at your age, to be taught how to behave yourselves.   1620
But there are chains, there is starvation with its pain,
excellent teachers of good manners to old men,
wise surgeons and exemplars. Look! Can you not see it?
Kick not at the goads for fear you hit them, and be hurt.

CHORUS LEADER

So then you, like a woman, waited the war out   1625
here in the house, shaming the master's bed with lust,
and planned against the lord of war this treacherous death?

AEGISTHUS

It is just such words as these will make you cry in pain.
Not yours the lips of Orpheus, no, quite otherwise—
his voice of rapture led all creatures in his train;   1630
you shall be led away, for babyish cries sobbed out
in rage. Once broken, you will be easier to deal with.

CHORUS LEADER

How shall you be lord of the men of Argos, you
who planned the murder of this man, yet could not dare
to act it out and cut him down with your own hand?   1635

AEGISTHUS

No, clearly the deception was the woman's part,
and I was suspect, that had hated him so long.
Still with his money I shall endeavor to control
the citizens. The mutinous man shall feel the yoke
drag at his neck, no oat-fed racehorse running free,   1640
but hunger, grim companion of the dark dungeon
shall see him trudging, broken to the hand at last.

CHORUS LEADER

But why, why then, you coward, could you not have slain
your man yourself? Why must it be his wife who killed,
to curse the country and the gods within the ground?   1645
Oh, can Orestes live, be somewhere in sunlight still?
Shall fate grown gracious ever bring him back again
in strength of hand to overwhelm these murderers?

AEGISTHUS

You shall learn then, since you stick to stubbornness of
    mouth and hand.

CHORUS LEADER°

Come on now, my trusty comrades: here is work for you
to do.   1650

AEGISTHUS

Come on now! Let every man clap fist upon his ready sword.

CHORUS LEADER

I as well am ready-handed; I am not afraid of death.

AEGISTHUS

Death you said and death it shall be; so I take up the word of
fate.

CLYTAEMESTRA

No, my dearest, dearest of all men, we have done enough. No
more
violence. Here is a monstrous harvest and a bitter reaping
time.   1655
There is pain enough already. Let us not be bloody now.
Honored gentlemen of Argos, go to your homes now and
give way°
to the stress of fate and season. We could not do otherwise
than we did. If this is the end of suffering, we can be content
broken as we are by the brute heel of angry destiny.   1660
Thus a woman speaks among you. Shall men deign to
understand?

AEGISTHUS

Yes, but think of these foolish lips that blossom° into leering
gibes;
think of the taunts they spit against me daring destiny and
power,
sober opinion lost in insults hurled against my majesty.

CHORUS LEADER

It was never the Argive way to grovel at a vile man's feet.   1665

AEGISTHUS

I shall not forget this; in the days to come I shall be there.

CHORUS LEADER

Nevermore, if god's guiding hand brings Orestes home again.

AEGISTHUS

Exiles feed on empty dreams of hope. I know it. I was one.

CHORUS LEADER

Have your way, gorge and grow fat, soil justice, while the
power is yours.

AEGISTHUS

You shall pay, make no mistake, for this foolishness.   1670

CHORUS LEADER

Crow and strut, brave cockerel by your hen; you have no
threats to fear.

CLYTAEMESTRA

Do not heed their empty yappings; come now, dearest, you
and I
have the power; we two shall bring good order to our house at
least.

(Exit Aegisthus and Clytaemestra into the palace.)

PROMETHEUS BOUND

AESCHYLUS
Translated by David Grene

INTRODUCTION TO AESCHYLUS' PROMETHEUS BOUND

The date of this play is unknown. On stylistic grounds, many scholars have concluded that it was not written by Aeschylus, or that it was left incomplete by him and finished by others, perhaps his playwright son, Euphorion. The other two tragedies which completed the trilogy are lost (only short fragments of them survive in ancient quotations), and the arrangement is disputed: their titles were *Prometheus Fire-Bearer* and *Prometheus Unbound*. It is not certain whether our play came first or second in order.

The story is taken from a well-known myth about Prometheus' dispute with Zeus in the early days after the creation of humankind, most famously narrated by the archaic Greek poet Hesiod. The play opens strikingly with the brutal fastening of Prometheus to the rock, but a great deal of the body of the play is taken up with the explanation, through the hero's conversations with others, of how this punishment has come about. In the great revolution of the young Olympian gods against the previous generation of divinities known as the Titans, Prometheus, himself a Titan, went over to the side of the Olympians; it is, he claims, thanks to his wise strategic advice that Olympian Zeus is now the master of the universe. But Prometheus outraged Zeus by befriending and aiding, against the plans of Zeus, the pitiful, rudimentary, experimental race of humans: most notably, he gave them fire and all kinds of technology. Therefore he is punished and, at the end of our play, is sunk beneath the earth, whence he will emerge (we are told) only to face the new torment of the eagle which Zeus will send to feed upon his liver. The sequel, *Prometheus Unbound*, of which some fragments remain, began with Prometheus suffering his new agony, before Heracles, the descendant of Io, frees him by killing the eagle. But we do not know how the eventual reconciliation of Prometheus with Zeus, confidently predicted in *Prometheus Bound*, was handled. It seems that the trilogy concluded with the installation of Prometheus as a god of cult and the establishment of the ritual torch race at Athens which is partly in his honor. But we cannot tell whether this was presented in the (totally lost) third play, *Prometheus Fire-Bearer*, or within *Prometheus Unbound* itself—in which case *Fire-Bearer* will have been the first play, preceding *Prometheus Bound*.

The most startling aspect of *Prometheus Bound* is the cruel and merciless part played by Zeus. Although he never appears, his motives seem plain, and they are described as those of a tyrant. Romantic poets such as Goethe and Shelley welcomed this story as a parable of human revolt against autocracy and established religion. But Prometheus, for all that he is the helper and champion of human beings, is nonetheless himself a god—and the ultimate reconciliation between him and the new ruler of Olympus is not to be forgotten.

PROMETHEUS BOUND

Characters   MIGHT, a henchman of Zeus

                VIOLENCE (nonspeaking character)

                HEPHAESTUS

                PROMETHEUS

                CHORUS of daughters of Ocean

                OCEAN

                IO, daughter of Inachus, the king of Argos

                HERMES

Scene: A bare and desolate crag in the Caucasus.

> *(Enter Might and Violence, followed by*
> *Hephaestus carrying blacksmith's tools.)*

MIGHT

This is the world's limit that we've come to;
the Scythian country, an unpeopled desert.
It's your job now, Hephaestus, to carry out
the commands the Father laid on you, to nail
this malefactor to the high craggy rocks   5
in fetters unbreakable of adamantine chain.
For it was your flower, the brilliance of fire
that enables all the arts, your flower he stole
and gave to humankind; this is the sin
for which he must pay the gods the penalty—
so that he may learn to accept the sovereignty   10
of Zeus and quit his human-loving ways.

HEPHAESTUS

Might and Violence, with you the command of Zeus
has found fulfilment; for you there is nothing
still left to tackle. But, for myself, I have not
the heart to bind a god who's my own kin
violently here on this wintry cliff.   15
Yet it's utterly required for me to have the heart
to do just that, for it is no light matter
to neglect or disrespect the Father's words.
              High-contriving Prometheus, son of Themis,
the goddess of straight counsel, this is not
of your will nor of mine; yet I shall nail you
to this crag in bonds of indissoluble bronze,   20
far from men. Here you shall neither hear
the voice nor see the form of any mortal.
You'll be grilled by the sun's bright fire and change the fair
bloom of your skin; then you'll be glad when night
comes with her mantle of stars and hides the sun's
light; but then the sun will scatter the frost   25
again at dawn. The pain of your present torture
will be there always to wear you down; for he
that can relieve it has not yet been born.
Such is the reward you reap for loving humans.
For you, a god, feared not the anger of gods,
but gave honor to mortals beyond what was just.   30
So in return, you'll guard this loveless rock—
standing, sleepless, never bending the knee:
many a groan and many a lamentation
you'll utter, but they will not help you; no,
the mind of Zeus is hard to soften with prayer,
and every ruler's harsh whose rule is new.   35

MIGHT

Come, why are you holding back? Why are you pitying—
in vain? Why is it that you do not hate a god

whom the gods hate most of all? Why don't you hate him,
since it was your honor that he betrayed to men?

HEPHAESTUS

Kinship has strange power, and our life together.

MIGHT

Yes. But to turn deaf ears to the Father's words—   40
how can that be? Do you not fear that more?

HEPHAESTUS

You are always pitiless, always full of ruthlessness.

MIGHT

There is no point singing dirges over him.
Don't labor uselessly at what doesn't help at all.

HEPHAESTUS

O handicraft of mine—that I deeply hate!   45

MIGHT

Why do you hate it? To speak simply, your craft
is in no way to blame for his present troubles.

HEPHAESTUS

Yet I wish this craft were allotted to someone else!

MIGHT

Everything has its burdens, except ruling
over the gods. For only Zeus is free.   50

HEPHAESTUS

I know—I can see that here! And I have no answer.

MIGHT

Hurry then. Throw the chain around him, so
the Father may not see you being slow.

HEPHAESTUS

There are the fetters, there: you can see them.

MIGHT

    Put them on his hands; now with the hammer, strike   55
    with all your strength; nail him to the rock.

HEPHAESTUS

    It is being done now. I am not idling at my work.

MIGHT

    Hammer it more; put in the wedge; leave nothing
    loose. He's clever at finding a way out
    even from hopeless difficulties.

HEPHAESTUS

    Look now, his arm is fixed immovably.   60

MIGHT

    Nail the other fast, that he may learn, for all
    his cleverness, that he's not as smart as Zeus.

HEPHAESTUS

    No one, save Prometheus, can justly blame me.

MIGHT

    Drive the obstinate jaw of the adamantine wedge
    right through his breast; drive it hard.   65

HEPHAESTUS

    Ah, Prometheus, I groan for your sufferings.

MIGHT

    Are you pitying again, and groaning for Zeus' enemies?
    Have a care, lest some day you may be pitying yourself.

HEPHAESTUS

    You see a sight that hurts the eye to see it.

MIGHT

    I see that he is getting what he deserves.   70
    Now cast the chest bands firmly around his sides.

HEPHAESTUS

    I am forced to do this; do not keep urging me.

MIGHT

Yes, I will urge you, and hound you on as well.
Get below now, and hoop his legs in strongly.

HEPHAESTUS

There now, the task is done. It's not taken long.   75

MIGHT

Hammer the piercing fetters with all your power,
for the overseer of our work is harsh.

HEPHAESTUS

Your looks and the refrain of your tongue are alike.

MIGHT

You can be softhearted. But do not blame
my stubbornness and harshness of temper.   80

HEPHAESTUS

Let us go. He has the harness on his limbs.

(Exit Hephaestus to the side.)

MIGHT   (To Prometheus.)

So now, play the insolent; now, plunder
the privileges of the gods and give them
to creatures of a day. What kind of help
can mortals offer to save you from these sufferings?
The gods misname you when they call you Forethought: 85
it's you yourself who need Forethought, by which
to extricate yourself from this contrivance.

(Might and Violence depart to the side. Prometheus is left alone.)

PROMETHEUS

Bright sky, springs of the rivers, swift-winged winds,
numberless laughter of the sea's waves, Earth,   90
mother of all, and all-seeing circle of the sun:
I call upon you all to see what I,
a god, suffer at the hands of gods.

[*chanting*]

        See with what kind of tortures
worn down I shall wrestle ten thousand
years of time—such are   95
the shameful shackles that he,
the new commander of the Blessed Ones,
has devised against me.
Ah, ah!
I groan for the present sorrow,
I groan for the sorrow to come.
When shall the time come
to ordain a limit to my sufferings?   100

[*speaking*]

But what am I saying? I have foreknowledge of
all that shall be; it's clearly known to me,
and none of these pains shall come as a surprise.
So must I bear, as lightly as I can,
the destiny that fate has given me;
for I know well that against necessity,
in all its strength, no one can fight and win.   105
I cannot speak about my fortune, cannot
hold my tongue either. It was mortals, humans,
to whom I gave great privileges, and
for that was yoked in this unyielding harness.
I hunted out the secret spring of fire   110
that filled the fennel stalk, which when revealed
became the teacher of each craft to men,
a great resource. This is the crime committed
for which I stand convicted, and I pay
nailed in my chains under the open sky.

[*singing*]

Ah! Ah!
What sound, what unseen smell approaches me,   115
god-sent, or mortal, or mingled?
Has someone come to earth's end

to look on my sufferings,
or wishing something else?

[chanting]
      You see me a wretched god in chains,
the enemy of Zeus, hated of all   120
the gods that enter Zeus's halls,
because of my excessive love for mortals.
    Ah, ah! What is that? The rustle
of birds' wings near? The air whispers   125
with the gentle strokes of wings.
Everything that comes toward me
is occasion for fear.

                    (The Chorus enters.)°

CHORUS [singing while Prometheus chants in response]
          STROPHE A
Fear not: this is a company of friends
that comes to your mountain with swift
rivalry of wings.   130
Scarcely had we persuaded our father's
mind, and the quick-bearing winds
speeded us hither. The sound
of stroke of iron rang through our cavern
in its depths, and it shook from us
shamefaced modesty; unsandaled
we have hastened on our chariot of wings.   135

PROMETHEUS
Ah, children of teeming Tethys
and of him who encircles all
the world with unsleeping stream,
father Ocean: 140
look, see with what chains
I am nailed on the craggy heights
of this ravine to keep a watch
that none would envy.

CHORUS

I see, Prometheus, and a mist of fear and tears
assails my eyes as I see your body   145
wasting away on these cliffs
in adamantine bonds of bitter shame.
For new are the steersmen that rule Olympus,
and new are the customs by which Zeus rules,
customs that have no justice to them,   150
but what was great before he brings to nothingness.

PROMETHEUS

I wish that he had hurled me
underneath the earth and underneath
the House of Hades, host to the dead—
yes, down to limitless Tartarus,
yes, though he bound me cruelly   155
in chains unbreakable,
so neither god nor any other being
might have found joy in gloating over me.
Now as I hang, the plaything of the winds,
my enemies can laugh at what I suffer.

CHORUS

STROPHE B

Who of the gods is so hard of heart   160
that he finds joy in this?
Who is there that does not feel
sorrow answering your pain—
save only Zeus? For he malignantly,
always cherishing a mind
that does not bend, has subdued the breed
of Ouranos, nor shall he cease   165
until either he satisfies his heart
or someone take the power from him—power that's hard to take!—
by some device of subtlety.

PROMETHEUS

Yes, there will come a day
when he will need me, me that now
am tortured in bonds and fetters—
he will need me then,
this president of the Blessed Ones—
to show him the new plot whereby he can be   170
despoiled of his throne and his power.
Then not with honeyed tongues
of persuasion will he enchant me;
he will not cow me with his threats
to tell him what I know,
until he frees me from my cruel chains   175
and pays me recompense for what I suffer.

CHORUS

You are stout of heart, unyielding
to the bitterness of pain.
You are free of tongue, too free.   180
But piercing fear has disturbed my mind;
your misfortunes frighten me.
Where and when is it fated
to see you reach the term, to see you reach
the harbor free of trouble at the last?
A disposition none can touch, a heart
that no persuasions soften—these are his,
the son of Cronus.   185

PROMETHEUS

I know that he's savage, his justice
a thing he keeps by his own standard;
yet that will of his shall melt
to softness in due course,
when he is broken in the way I know;
and though his temper now

is oak-hard, it will be softened: 190
eagerly he'll come to meet
my eagerness, to join
in amity and union with me—
one day he will come.

CHORUS LEADER [*speaking*]
Reveal it all to us: tell us the story
of what the charge was on which Zeus caught you
and punished you so cruelly with such dishonor.   195
Tell us, if telling will not injure you.

PROMETHEUS [*speaking*]
To speak of this is bitterness. To keep silent
bitter no less; and every way is misery.
When first the gods began their angry quarrel,
and god matched god in growing faction, some   200
eager to drive old Cronus from his throne
so Zeus might rule—the fools!—others again
eager that Zeus should never be their king,
I then with the best counsel tried to win
the Titans, sons of Ouranos and Earth,   205
but failed. They would have none of crafty schemes
and in their savage arrogance of spirit
thought they would lord it easily by force.
But she that was my mother, Themis, Earth—
she is but one although her names are many—   210
had prophesied to me how it would be,
just as it was determined, and she said,
"Not by strength nor overmastering force
must victory be decided, but the conquest
must be by guile." This is what I told them,
but they wouldn't even consider it at all.   215
        Then with those things before me it seemed best
to take my mother and join Zeus's side,
and he was just as willing as we were;
thanks to my plans the dark receptacle

of Tartarus conceals the ancient Cronus,   220
him and his allies. These were the services
I rendered to this tyrant and these pains
the payment he has given me in return.
This is a sickness rooted and inherent
in the nature of a tyranny:
that the one who holds it doesn't trust his friends.   225
    But you have asked on what particular
charge he now tortures me: this I will tell you.
As soon as he ascended to the throne
that was his father's, straightway he assigned
to the several gods their several privileges   230
and portioned out the power; but to the unhappy
breed of mankind he gave no heed, intending
to blot the race out and create a new one.
No one opposed these plans save I: I dared.
I rescued men from shattering destruction   235
that would have carried them to Hades' house
and therefore I am tortured on this rock,
a bitterness to suffer, and piteous
to see. I gave priority to mortals
in pity, but found none of it for myself.
Instead I'm being disciplined like this,   240
pitilessly, a spectacle that brings
shame and dishonor to the name of Zeus.

CHORUS LEADER
Iron-minded and made of stone would be indeed,
Prometheus, anyone who did not sympathize
with your sufferings. I would not have chosen
to see them, and now I see, my heart is pained.   245

PROMETHEUS
Yes, to my friends I am pitiable to see.

CHORUS LEADER
Did you perhaps go further than you have told us?

PROMETHEUS

I caused mortals to cease foreseeing death.

CHORUS LEADER

What cure did you provide against that sickness?

PROMETHEUS

I placed in them blind hopes.   250

CHORUS LEADER

                                    That was indeed
a great benefaction that you gave to mortals.

PROMETHEUS

Besides this, I also gave them fire.

CHORUS LEADER

And do creatures of a day now possess bright fire?

PROMETHEUS

Yes, and from it they shall learn many crafts.

CHORUS LEADER

Then these are the charges on which—   255

PROMETHEUS

Zeus tortures me and gives me no respite.

CHORUS LEADER

Is there no limit set to end your pain?

PROMETHEUS

None save when it will seem good to Zeus.

CHORUS LEADER

How will it ever seem good to him? What hope
is there? Do you not see how you have erred?   260
It is not pleasant for me to say you've erred,
and for you it is a pain to hear. But let us speak
no more of this; instead, look for some means
of deliverance and release from your torment.

PROMETHEUS

It is an easy thing for one whose foot
is on the outside of calamity
to give advice and to rebuke the sufferer.
I knew all this, and all that I did wrong   265
I did on purpose; I shall not deny it.
In helping mortals I brought pain on myself;
but yet I did not think that with such tortures
as these I should be withered on these cliffs,
up high, alone, on this deserted hillside.   270
     But do not sorrow for my present suffering;
alight on earth and hear what is to come
so you may know it all, right to the end.
I beg you, alight and join your sorrow with mine:
misfortune wanders everywhere, and settles   275
now upon one and now upon another.

CHORUS [chanting]
Willing our ears,
that hear you cry to us, Prometheus.
Now with light foot I'll leave
the rushing car and sky,
the holy path of birds,   280
and approach the rugged earth:
I long to hear the story
of your troubles to the end.

(*The Chorus exits.° Enter Ocean, riding on a winged sea monster.*)

OCEAN [chanting]
I come to my destination
completing a long journey,   285
to visit you, Prometheus.
I direct my swift-winged bird
with the mind alone, no bridle.
In my heart I share the pain
for your misfortunes; you know that.

I think that it is kinship
that makes me feel them so.   290
Besides, apart from kinship,
there's no one that I hold
in higher estimation than you.
This you soon shall know for sure
and know beside that in me
there is no mere word-kindness;
tell me how I can help you,   295
and you will never say
that you have any friend
more loyal to you than Ocean.

PROMETHEUS

What do I see? Have you, too, come to stare
in wonder at this great display, my torture?
How did you have the courage to come here   300
to this land, mother of iron, leaving the stream
called after you and the rock-roofed, self-established
caverns? Was it to feast your eyes upon
the spectacle of my suffering and join
in pity for my pain? Now look and see
the sight, this friend of Zeus, that helped set up   305
his monarchy, and see what agonies
twist me, by his instructions!

OCEAN [*now speaking*]

                                        Yes, I see,
Prometheus, and I want, indeed I do,
to advise you for the best, for all your cleverness.
Know yourself and reform your ways to new ways,   310
for new is he that rules among the gods.
But if you throw about such angry words,
words that are whetted swords, soon Zeus will hear you,
even though his seat aloft is far removed,
and then your present multitude of pains
will seem like child's play. My poor friend, give up

this angry mood of yours and look for ways   315
of freeing yourself from these troubles. Maybe
what I say seems to you both old and commonplace;
but this is what you pay, Prometheus, for
that tongue of yours which talked so high and haughty:
you are not yet humble; still you do not yield
to your misfortunes, and you wish, indeed,   320
to add some more to them; now, if you follow
me as your teacher, you will not rear and kick
against the rider's whip, seeing that our king,
ruling alone, is harsh and sends accounts
to no one's audit for the deeds he does.
            Now I will go and try if I can free you,   325
so you be quiet; do not talk so much.
Since your mind is so subtle, don't you know
that a thoughtless tongue is subject to correction?

PROMETHEUS

    I envy you, that you stand so clear of blame,   330
yet shared and dared in everything with me!
Now let me be, and do not get involved.
Do what you will, you'll never persuade him!
He is not easily won over: look,
take care you are not harmed for your journey here.

OCEAN

    By nature you're much better at advising   335
others than yourself. I take my cue
from deeds, not words. Do not restrain me now
when I am eager to go to Zeus. I'm sure,
I'm sure that he will grant this favor to me,
to free you from these torments you have now.

PROMETHEUS

    I thank you and will never cease; for eagerness   340
is not what you are wanting in. Don't trouble,
for you will trouble to no purpose, and no help

to me—even if you really do want to trouble.
No, rest yourself, keep out of the way;
just because I'm unlucky I would not,   345
for that, have everyone else be unlucky too.
No, for my heart is sore already when
I think about my brothers' fortunes—Atlas,
who stands to westward of the world, supporting
the pillar of earth and heaven on his shoulders,   350
a load beyond all bearing; also Typhon,
the earthborn dweller in that Cilician cave,
whom I saw and pitied, a hundred-headed monster,
dreadful, yet conquered and brought low by force.°
Once against all the gods he stood, opposed,   355
hissing out terror from his grim jaws; his eyes
flashed gorgon-glaring lightning as he thought
to smash the sovereign tyranny of Zeus.
But down upon him came the unsleeping bolt
of Zeus, the lightning-breathing flame, onrushing,
which hurled him from his high aspiring boasts.   360
Struck to the heart, his strength was blasted dead
and burnt to ashes; now a sprawling mass
useless he lies, hard by the narrow seaway
pressed down beneath the roots of Aetna. High   365
above him on the mountain peak the smith
Hephaestus works at the anvil. Yet one day
there shall burst out rivers of fire, devouring
with savage jaws the fertile, level plains
of Sicily with their fair fruits; such wrath
boiling with weapons of fire-breathing surf,   370
an unapproachable torrent, shall Typhon vomit,
though Zeus's lightning's left him but a cinder.
              But all of this you know: you don't need me
to be your teacher; reassure yourself
as you know how—this cup I shall drain myself   375
until the high mind of Zeus shall cease from anger.

OCEAN

So do you not know, Prometheus, that words
are healers of a temper that is sick?

PROMETHEUS

Yes, if one tries at just the right moment
to soften the heart, and doesn't violently
seek to reduce the anger that's still swelling.   380

OCEAN

Tell me, what danger do you see for me
in loyalty to you, and courage therein?

PROMETHEUS

I see just useless effort—and silly good nature.

OCEAN

Allow me then to be sick of this sickness, since
it's profitable, if one's wise, to seem foolish.   385

PROMETHEUS

This shall seem to be *my* fault, more than yours.

OCEAN

Clearly your words send me home again.

PROMETHEUS

Yes, lest your grieving for me bring you enemies.

OCEAN

The one who newly sits on the all-powerful throne?

PROMETHEUS

Yes, his is a heart you should beware of vexing.   390

OCEAN

Your own misfortune's my teacher, Prometheus.

PROMETHEUS

Off with you, then! Begone—keep your present mind.

OCEAN

These words fall on very responsive ears.
Already my four-legged bird is pawing the air,
the level track of heaven, with his wings,   395
and he'll gladly bend the knee in his own stable.

(Exit Ocean. The Chorus reenters from the side.)°

CHORUS [singing]
STROPHE A

I cry aloud, Prometheus, and lament your bitter fate,
my tender eyes are trickling tears,
their fountains wet my cheek.   400
With these cruel things done by his own private laws,
Zeus the tyrant shows his haughtiness
of temper toward the gods that were of old.   405

ANTISTROPHE A

Now all the earth has cried aloud, lamenting:
they lament what was magnificent of old,
in sorrow for your fall and for your brethren's fall.°   410
All the mortals who in holy Asia hold
their stablished habitation, all lament
in sympathy for your most grievous woes,

STROPHE B

and the dwellers in the land of Colchis,   415
maidens, fearless in the fight,
and the host of Scythia, living
round the lake Maeotis, living
on the edges of the world,

ANTISTROPHE B

and Arabia's flower of warriors   420
and the craggy fortress keepers
near Caucasian mountains, fighters
terrible, crying for battle,
brandishing sharp-pointed spears.

Only one other of the Titans have I seen   425
before this day, in torture and in bonds
unbreakable, god though he was,
Atlas, whose strength and might
were surpassing; now he bends his back
and groans beneath the load of earth and heaven.°   430

The wave cries out as it breaks into surf;
the depth cries out, lamenting you; the dark
Hades, the hollow underneath the world,
sullenly groans below; the springs
of sacred flowing rivers all lament
the pain and pity of your suffering.   435

PROMETHEUS

Don't think I'm silent out of pride or stubbornness:
in self-awareness my heart is gnawed away
to see myself insulted as I am.
Yet who was it but I who distributed   440
their honors to these new gods? I'll say no more
of this; you know it all; but hear what troubles
there were among mortals, how I found them mindless
but made them intelligent and masters of their minds.
I'll tell you this, not blaming human beings,   445
but to explain the goodwill of my gifts.
For humans in the beginning had eyes but saw
to no purpose; they had ears but did not hear.
Like the shapes of dreams they dragged through their long
   lives
and muddled everything haphazardly.   450
They did not know how to build brick houses
to face the sun; nor how to work in wood.
They lived beneath the earth like swarming ants,
in sunless caves. For them there was no secure
token for telling winter or flowering spring,   455

nor summer with its crops; and all they did
they did without intelligent calculation
until I showed them the rising of the stars,
and the settings, hard to observe. And I invented
numbers for them, preeminent among all skills.
and the combining of written letters as a means   460
of remembering all things, the Muses' mother,
skilled in craft. It was I who first yoked beasts
to be slaves in harness and under pack saddles,°
as substitutes for humans in hard tasks;
and I harnessed to the carriage obedient horses,   465
the crowning pride of wealth and luxury.
It was I and none other who discovered ships,
sail-winged wagons that bear men over the sea.
Such—to my misery—were the devices which
I discovered for mortals, but I have no clever means   470
to rid myself of my own present affliction.

CHORUS LEADER
You have suffered terribly. Bewildered in your mind
you are astray, and like a bad doctor who
has fallen sick, you have lost heart not finding
by what drugs your own illness might be cured.   475

PROMETHEUS
If you hear the rest you will marvel even more
at the crafts and the resources I contrived.
Greatest was this: when one of mankind fell sick
there was no defense for him—neither healing food
nor drink nor unguent; for lack of cures they wasted,   480
until I showed them the blending of mild remedies
with which they drive away all kinds of sickness.
    The many ways of prophecy I charted;
I was the first to judge what out of dreams
came truly real; and for mankind I gave meaning   485
to ominous cries, hard of interpretation,

and to the significance of road encounters.
The flight of hook-taloned birds I analyzed,
which of them were in nature propitious
and which unlucky; what habits each species has,   490
what are their hates and loves and affiliations.
    Also I taught of the smoothness of the entrails
and what color the bile should have to please the gods,
and the dappled symmetry of the liver lobe.   495
It was I who burned the thigh bones wrapped in fat
and the long shank bone; I set mortals on the road
to the murky craft of divination, making
the flaming signs, once dim, now clear to see.
So much for these things. Then beneath the earth   500
those hidden blessings, copper, iron, silver,
and gold—who can claim to have discovered them before me?
No one, I am sure, who wants to speak to the purpose.
In one short sentence understand it all: 505
all human arts come from Prometheus.

CHORUS LEADER
    Well, don't help mortals beyond due occasion
    while careless of yourself in your own troubles.
    I am of good hope that you, freed of these bonds,
    will one day be no less in power than Zeus.   510

PROMETHEUS
    Not yet has fate that brings all things to pass
    determined this. First I must be tormented
    by ten thousand pangs and agonies, as I am now,
    before I can escape my chains.
    Craft is far weaker than necessity.

CHORUS LEADER
    Who then is the steersman of necessity?   515

PROMETHEUS
    The three-formed Fates and the remembering Furies.

CHORUS LEADER

And is Zeus, then, weaker than these?

PROMETHEUS

Yes,

for he too cannot escape what is fated.

CHORUS LEADER

But what is fated for Zeus save eternal rule?

PROMETHEUS

You cannot know that yet; do not entreat me.   520

CHORUS LEADER

This must be some solemn secret that you're hiding.

PROMETHEUS

Think of some other story; this one's not seasonable
to utter, it must be wholly hidden.
For only by so keeping it can I
escape my shameful bonds and agonies.   525

CHORUS [*singing*]

STROPHE A

May Zeus never, Zeus that controls
the whole universe, oppose
his power against my mind;
may I never be lazy
or slow to give my worship at   530
the sacrificial feasts
when the bulls are killed beside
the quenchless stream of father Ocean;
may I never sin in word;
may these precepts still abide
in my mind nor melt away.   535

ANTISTROPHE A

It is a sweet thing to draw out

a long, long life in cheerful hopes,
and feed the spirit in the bright
benignity of happiness;
but I shudder when I see you   540
wasted with ten thousand pains,°
all because you did not tremble
at the name of Zeus: your mind
was yours, not his, and at its bidding
you regarded mortal beings
too high, Prometheus.

STROPHE B

Kindness that can't be requited—tell me, where   545
is the help in that, my friend? What support
in creatures of a day? You did not see
the feebleness that draws its breath in gasps,
a dreamlike feebleness by which the race
of humans is held in bondage, a blind prisoner.   550
So the plans of mortals shall never
surpass the ordered law of Zeus.

ANTISTROPHE B

This I have learned while I looked on your fortunes,
these deadly pains of yours, Prometheus.
A dirge for you came to my lips, so different
from the other song I sang to crown your marriage,   555
in honor of the bath and of the bed,
upon the day you won her with your gifts°
to be your wife—my sister, Hesione,
and so you brought her home to share your bed.   560

(Enter Io from the side, with horns like an ox on her head.)

IO [*chanting*]

What land is this? What race of men?
Who is it I see here being tortured
in rocky bondage? What is the crime

he's paying for? Tell me, to what part
of the world have my wanderings brought me?   565

[*singing*]
O, O, O,
there it is again, there again — it stings me,
the gadfly, the ghost of earthborn Argus;
keep it away, keep it away!
I'm frightened when I see the shape of Argus,
Argus the herdsman with ten thousand eyes.
He stalks me with his crafty eyes; he died,
but the earth didn't hide him; still he comes   570
even from the depths of the underworld to hunt me:
he drives me starving by the sands of the sea.

STROPHE A

The loud reed pipes, glued with wax,
drone their sleep-giving melody: 575
O, O, O!
Where am I brought by my far-wandering wanderings?
Son of Cronus, what fault, what fault
did you find in me that you should yoke me
to a harness of misery like this, O, O,
that you should torture me so to madness   580
driven in fear of the gadfly?
Burn me with fire; hide me in earth; cast me away
to monsters of the deep for food; but do not
begrudge me the granting of this prayer, King.
Enough have my much-wandering wanderings   585
exercised me; I cannot find
a way to escape my troubles.
Do you hear the voice of the cow-horned girl?

PROMETHEUS [*speaking*]
    Surely I hear the voice of the gadfly-haunted
    daughter of Inachus, who fired with love   590
    the heart of Zeus and now through Hera's hate
    is violently driven on courses overlong.

IO [*still singing*]

How is it you speak my father's name?
Tell me, who are you? Who are you? Oh
who are you that so exactly accosts me by name?   595
You have spoken of the disease that the gods have sent to me
which wastes me away, pricking with goads,
so that I am moving always
tortured and hungry, wild bounding.
Quick-sped I come,   600
a victim of Hera's jealous plots.
Who has been so wretched, O, O,
before me, as to suffer as I do?
But declare to me clearly
what I have still to suffer, what would avail   605
against my sickness, what drug would cure it.
Tell me, if you know:
tell me, declare it to this unlucky, wandering girl.

PROMETHEUS

I shall tell you clearly all that you would know,
weaving no riddles, but simply, in plain words,   610
as it is just to open one's lips to friends.
You see Prometheus, giver of fire to men.

IO [*now speaking*]

You that have shown yourself a shared blessing
to all mankind, unhappy Prometheus,
for what are you being punished in this way?

PROMETHEUS

I have just now ceased from telling my mournful tale.   615

IO

Then will you grant me this favor?

PROMETHEUS

                            Say what it is
you are requesting; you will learn it all.

[93] PROMETHEUS BOUND

IO

Tell who it was that nailed you to the cliff.

PROMETHEUS

The plan was Zeus', but it was Hephaestus' hand.

IO

What was the offense for which this is the punishment?   620

PROMETHEUS

It's enough that I have told you clearly so far.

IO

In addition, then, indicate to me what date
will be the limit of my wanderings.

PROMETHEUS

Better for you not to know this than to know it.

IO

Don't hide from me what I am due to suffer.   625

PROMETHEUS

It's not that I begrudge you this favor that you ask.

IO

Why then delay to tell me everything?

PROMETHEUS

No grudging, but I hesitate to break your spirit.

IO

Do not have more thought for me than I want myself.

PROMETHEUS

Since you're so eager, I must speak; hear me.   630

CHORUS LEADER

Not yet. Give to me, too, a share of pleasure.
First let us question her about her sickness,
and let her tell us of her ruinous fortunes.
Then she can learn from you her sufferings to come.

PROMETHEUS

    It is your task, Io, to gratify these spirits,   635
    who are moreover your father's sisters. For
    wailing and lamenting one's ill fortune,
    when one will win a tear from those who listen,
    is well worthwhile.

IO

    I know not how I should distrust you; clearly   640
    you will hear all you want to know from me.
    Yet I'm ashamed to speak about that storm,
    god-sent, that ruin of my beauty, and
    how it came upon me. There were constant
    night visions that kept haunting me and coming   645
    into my maiden chamber and exhorting
    with winning words, "O maiden greatly blessed,
    why are you still a virgin, you who might
    make marriage with the greatest? Zeus is stricken
    with desire for you; he's afire to try the act
    of love with you; do not disdain the bed   650
    of Zeus. Go, child, to Lerna's grassy meadow,
    to where your father's flocks and cattle stand
    so that Zeus's eye may cease from longing for you."
    With such dreams I was cruelly beset   655
    night after night until I took the courage
    to tell my father of my nightly dreams.
    He sent to Pytho many an embassy
    and to Dodona seeking to discover
    what deed or word of his might please the gods;   660
    but those he sent came back with riddling oracles
    dark and beyond the power of understanding.
    At last the word came clear to Inachus
    charging him plainly that he cast me out
    of home and country, drive me out unsupervised   665
    to wander to the limits of the world;
    if he should not obey, the oracle said,

the fire-faced thunderbolt would come from Zeus
and wipe out his whole race. These were the oracles
of Loxias, and Inachus obeyed them.
He drove me out and shut his doors against me   670
with tears on both our parts, but Zeus's bridle
compelled him to do this against his will.
Immediately my form and mind were changed
and all distorted; as you see, with horns,
pricked on by the sharp-biting gadfly, leaping   675
in frenzied jumps I ran beside the river
of Cerchnea, good to drink, and Lerna's spring.
The earth-born herdsman Argus followed me
whose fierceness knew no limits, and he spied
after my tracks with all his hundred eyes.
Then an unlooked-for doom, descending suddenly,   680
took him from life; I, driven by the gadfly,
that god-sent scourge, am driven always onward
from one land to another. That is my story.
If you can tell me what remains for me,
tell me, and do not out of pity try
to soothe me with kindly lies; there is no sickness   685
more shameful in my view than made-up words.

CHORUS [*singing*]
   Hold! Keep away! Alas!
   never did I think that such strange
   words would come to my ears;
   never did I think such intolerable   690
   sufferings, an offense to the eye,
   shameful and frightening, so
   would chill my soul with a double-edged point.
   Ah, ah, what a fate!
   I shudder when I look on Io's fortune.   695

PROMETHEUS
   You groan already; you are full of fear too soon:
   wait till you hear besides what's still to come.

CHORUS LEADER
  Speak, tell us to the end. For the sick it is sweet to know
  beforehand clearly the pain that still remains.

PROMETHEUS
  The first request you made of me you gained   700
  lightly: from her you wished to hear the story
  of what she suffered. Now hear what still remains,
  what sufferings this girl must yet endure
  from Hera. Do you listen, child of Inachus,   705
  hear and lay up my words within your heart
  so you may know the limits of your journey.
  First turn to the sun's rising and walk on
  over the fields no plough has broken; then
  you will come to the nomad Scythians, who live
  in wicker houses built on well-wheeled wagons,
  aloft; they are armed with bows that strike from far.   710
  Do not draw near them; rather let your feet
  skirt the rocky coast where the waves moan,
  and pass through their country; on your left there live
  the Chalybes who work with iron: these   715
  you must beware of; for they are not gentle,
  not people whom a stranger dare approach.
  Then you will come to the River Insolence
  that well deserves its name, but do not cross it—
  it is not a stream that can be easily forded—
  until you come to Caucasus itself,
  the highest of mountains, where the river's strength   720
  gushes from its summit. So you must
  cross its peaks, the neighbors of the stars,
  and take the road southward until you reach
  the man-hating Amazons, who one day
  shall live around Thermodon in Themiscyra   725
  where Salmydessus stands, that rocky cape,
  hostile to sailors, stepmother of ships.
  The Amazons will set you on your way

and gladly; you will reach Cimmeria,   730
the isthmus, at the narrows of the lake.
Leave this with a bold heart and then traverse
the channel of Maeotis, and hereafter
for all time men shall talk about your crossing,
and they shall call the place for you Cow's-Ford.
Leave Europe's mainland then, and enter Asia.   735

(To the Chorus.)

Do you not think the tyrant of the gods
is equally brutal in all the things he does?
He is a god, yet sought to lie in love
with this girl who's mortal, and on her he's brought
this curse of wanderings. Bitter indeed, poor girl,
you've found this suitor for your favors. Yet   740
you still must think of all that I have told you
as only the prelude.

IO

Oh, oh!

PROMETHEUS

Again, you are crying and lamenting: what
will you do when you hear of the evils yet to come?

CHORUS LEADER

Is there more suffering to come that you must tell her?   745

PROMETHEUS

A wintry sea of agony and ruin.

IO

What good is life to me then? Why do I not throw
myself at once from this rough crag, to strike
the ground and find release from all my troubles?   750
It would be better to die once for all
than suffer all one's days.

PROMETHEUS

You'd find it hard to bear these trials of mine,
since for me death is not decreed at all.
Death would be indeed release from pain;
but for me there is no limit of suffering set   755
till Zeus shall fall from power.

IO

                                    And is that possible?
You mean that Zeus' rule might one day fall?

PROMETHEUS

You would be glad, I think, to see that outcome.

IO

Of course, since it's from Zeus I suffer so.

PROMETHEUS

Then know that this is truly how things are.°   760

IO

Who will despoil him of his sovereign scepter?

PROMETHEUS

His own light-witted decisions will undo him.

IO

How? Tell me, if there is no harm to telling.

PROMETHEUS

He'll make a marriage that one day he'll regret.

IO

With god or mortal? Tell me, if it may be told.   765

PROMETHEUS

Why ask what marriage? That is not to be spoken.

IO

Is it from his wife that he shall lose his throne?

PROMETHEUS

Yes, she'll bear him a son mightier than his father.

IO

And has he no escape from this downfall?

PROMETHEUS

None, save myself—if I'm freed from my chains.   770

IO

But who is there to free you, against Zeus's will?

PROMETHEUS

It has to be one of your own descendants.

IO

What, shall a child of mine free you from torment?

PROMETHEUS

Yes, in the thirteenth generation to come.

IO

No longer can I grasp your prophecy.   775

PROMETHEUS

Then do not seek to learn your own troubles further.

IO

Don't offer me the gift and then withhold it.

PROMETHEUS

I'll give you then just one of the two stories.

IO

Which stories? Say, and let me have the choice.

PROMETHEUS

Yes, I will give that to you: either to tell you   780
clearly the rest of your troubles, or my deliverer.

CHORUS LEADER

Please, grant her the one and grant me the other favor;
don't disappoint us. Tell her what remains

of her wanderings in the future; and tell us
of your deliverer. That is what I want.   785

PROMETHEUS

Since you have so much eagerness, I will not
refuse to tell you all that you have asked me.
First to you, Io, I shall tell the tale
of your sad wanderings, rich in groans—inscribe
the story in the tablets of your mind.

    When you shall cross the channel that divides   790
Europe from Asia, turn to the rising sun,
and cross the sun-scorched plains, that waveless sea,°
until you arrive into the Gorgon land
and the flat stretches of Cisthene's country.
There live the ancient maids, children of Phorcys:
three swan-formed hags, with but one common eye,   795
single-toothed monsters, such as nowhere else
the sun's rays look on nor the moon by night.
Near are their winged sisters, the three Gorgons,
with snakes to bind their hair up, mortal-hating—
no mortal that looks on them shall still draw breath—   800
this is the garrison I tell you of.
Hear, too, of yet another gruesome sight,
the sharp-toothed hounds of Zeus, that have no bark,
the griffins—beware of them!—and the host
of one-eyed Arimaspians, horse-riding,   805
that live around the waters that flow with gold,
of the River Pluto: do not go near them.
A land far off, a nation of black people,
these you shall come to, men who live hard by
the fountain of the sun where is the river
Aethiops—travel by its banks along   810
to a cataract where from the Bybline hills
the Nile pours its holy, healthful waters.
This river shall be your guide to the three-cornered
land of Nilotis, and there, by fate's decree,

there, Io, you shall find your distant home,   815
a colony for you and your descendants.
If anything of this is still obscure
or difficult, ask me again and learn
clearly: I have more leisure than I wish.

CHORUS LEADER
If there is anything further or left over
you have to tell her of her deadly traveling,
tell it. If that is all, grant us in turn
the favor we asked for earlier. You remember?   820

PROMETHEUS
The limit of her wanderings she now
has heard, complete; but so that she may know
that she has not been listening to no purpose
I shall recount what she endured before   825
she came to us here: this I give as pledge,
a witness to the good faith of my words.
        The great part of the story I omit
and come to the last stage of your wanderings.
When you had come to the Molossian plains
around the steep ridge of Dodona, where   830
the oracular seat is of Thesprotian Zeus,
the talking oaks, a wonder past belief:
by them full clearly, in no riddling terms,
you were hailed Zeus' glorious wife-to-be.
Does any of this wake sweet memories?   835
Then, goaded by the gadfly, on you hastened
by the shoreline path to the great Gulf of Rhea.
But then in backward course, as if storm-driven,
you had to reverse your tracks; in time to come
that inlet of the sea shall bear your name
and shall be called Ionian, a memorial   840
to all men of your journeying; these are proofs
for you, of how my mind sees something farther
than what is visible.

(To the Chorus.)

For what is left,
to you and to her this I shall say in common,
taking up again the track of my old tale.   845
There is a city, on the furthest edge of land,
Canobus, near the mouth and issuing point
of the Nile: it's there that Zeus shall restore your mind,°
touching you with a hand that brings no fear,
and through that touch alone shall come your healing.
You shall bear Epaphus, dark of skin, his name   850
recalling Zeus's touch and his begetting.
This Epaphus shall reap the fruit of all
the land that is watered by the broad-flowing Nile.
From him five generations, and again
to Argos they shall come, against their will,
in number fifty, women, fleeing from
a marriage with their cousins; but these cousins,   855
their hearts with lust aflutter, just like hawks
barely outdistanced by fleeing doves, will come
hunting a marriage that's not theirs to hunt;
the gods shall grudge the men these women's bodies,
and the Pelasgian earth shall welcome them°   860
in death, for death shall claim them in a fight
where women strike in the dark, a murderous vigil.
Each wife shall rob her husband of his life
dipping in blood her two-edged sword; even so
may Cypris come, too, upon my enemies.
But one of these girls, softened by love's charms,   865
will spare her bedfellow, her purpose blunted;
and she shall make her choice—to bear the name
of coward and not murderer, and she
shall bear in Argos a family of kings.
To tell this clearly needs a longer story,   870
but from her seed shall spring a man renowned
for archery, and he shall set me free.

Such was the prophecy which ancient Themis
my Titan mother opened up to me;
but how and by what means it shall come true   875
would take too long to tell, and if you heard,
the knowledge would not profit you.

IO [*chanting*]
    Eleleu, eleleu!
    It grabs me again, the twitching spasm,
    the mind-destroying madness, burning me up,
    as the gadfly's sting pricks like fire;°   880
    my heart in its fear knocks on my breast.
    There's a dazing whirl in my eyes as I run
    out of my course driven by the wild winds
    of maddening frenzy; my tongue ungoverned
    babbles, the words in a thick muddy flow
    crash into the waves of hateful ruin   885
    without aim or sense.

                                        (*Exit Io to the side.*)

CHORUS [*singing*]
                    STROPHE A
    A wise man indeed he was
    that first in judgment weighed this word
    and gave it tongue: the best by far
    it is to marry in one's rank and station;   890
    let no one working with his hands aspire
    to marriage with those lifted high in pride
    because of wealth or ancestral glory.

                    ANTISTROPHE A
    Never, never may you see me,
    O you Fates, drawing close°   895
    to the bed of Zeus, to share it as his partner,
    nor ever may I be joined with a god for my wooer.
    I feel dread when I see Io, hating her husband,
    her virginity ravaged, in bitter wandering
    because of Hera's fierce wrath.   900

But when a match has equal partners
then I fear not; may the eye
inescapable of the mighty gods
not look on me with desire.
That is a fight that none can fight, a fruitful
source of fruitlessness. I would not
know what I could do; I cannot see   905
how I would escape the plans of Zeus.

PROMETHEUS

Yet shall this Zeus, for all his arrogance,
be humble yet: such is the match he plans,
a union that shall drive him from his power
and from his throne, out of the sight of all.   910
So shall at last the final consummation
be brought about of father Cronus' curse
which he, driven from his ancient throne, invoked
against the son deposing him; no one
of all the gods save I alone can tell
a way for him to avoid such troubles: I
do know this, and how. So let him confidently   915
sit on his throne and trust his heavenly thunder
and brandish in his hand his fiery bolt;
nothing shall all of this avail against
a humiliating and intolerable fall.
Such is the wrestler that Zeus is setting up   920
against himself, a monster hard to fight.
This enemy shall find a fire to best
the lightning bolt, a thunderclap to excel
the thunderclap of Zeus; and he shall shatter
Poseidon's trident, with quakes on sea and land.   925
So, in his crashing fall shall Zeus discover
how far apart are rule and slavery.

CHORUS LEADER

What you want for Zeus is what you're stating as fact.

PROMETHEUS

They are my wishes, yet what shall come to pass.

CHORUS LEADER

So should we expect someone to conquer Zeus?   930

PROMETHEUS

Yes; Zeus will suffer worse than I do now.

CHORUS LEADER

Have you no fear of uttering such words?

PROMETHEUS

Why should I fear, since death is not my fate?

CHORUS LEADER

But he might give you pain still worse than this.

PROMETHEUS

Then let him do so; all this I expect.   935

CHORUS LEADER

Wise are the worshippers of Necessity.

PROMETHEUS

Worship, pray; flatter whatever king
is king today; but I care less than nothing
for Zeus. Let him do just as he likes;   940
let him be king for his short time: he won't
be king of the gods for long.
                             But look, here comes
the footman of Zeus, that fetch-and-carry messenger
of the new king. Certainly he has come here
with news for us.

                                   (Enter Hermes from the side.)

HERMES

                 You, subtle spirit, you
bitter and overbitter, you that sinned   945
against the immortals, giving honor to

the creatures of a day, you thief of fire:
the Father has commanded you to say
what marriage of his is this you brag about
that shall drive him from power—and declare it
in detail and no riddles. You, Prometheus,
don't cause me a double journey; you can see   950
that Zeus is not softhearted in such matters.

PROMETHEUS

Your speech is pompous sounding, full of pride,
as fits the lackey of the gods. You are young
and young your rule, and you think the citadel   955
in which you live is free from sorrow. From it
have I not seen two previous tyrants fall?
The third, who now is king, I shall see too
fall, of the three most suddenly, most dishonored.
Do you think that I will cower before these gods,   960
—so new—and tremble? I am far from that.
Hurry away, back on the road you came.
You shall learn nothing that you ask of me.

HERMES

By previous obstinacy just like this
you've brought yourself to these your present torments.   965

PROMETHEUS

Be sure of this: when I measure my misfortune
against your slavery, I would not change.

HERMES

It is better, I suppose, to be a slave
to this rock, than Zeus's trusted messenger!

PROMETHEUS

.   .   .   .
Thus should one insult the insolent!°   970

HERMES

You seem to revel in your present state.

PROMETHEUS

Revel? I wish my enemies reveled so—
and you are one that I surely count among them.

HERMES

Oh, you would blame me too for your calamity?

PROMETHEUS

In a single word, I hate all of the gods   975
that unjustly returned me ill for good.

HERMES

Your words declare you mad, and mad indeed.

PROMETHEUS

Yes, if it's madness to detest my enemies.

HERMES

No one could bear you if you were successful.

PROMETHEUS

Alas!

HERMES

                        Alas? Zeus does not know that phrase.   980

PROMETHEUS

But time in its aging course teaches all things.

HERMES

Yet you have not yet learned a wise discretion.

PROMETHEUS

True: or I wouldn't be speaking to a servant.

HERMES

It seems you will not grant the Father's wish.

PROMETHEUS

I should be glad, indeed, to requite his kindness!   985

HERMES

You mock me like a child!

PROMETHEUS

             And are you not
a child, and sillier than a child, to think
that I should tell you anything? There's not
a torture or device of any kind
which Zeus can use to make me speak these things,   990
till these atrocious shackles have been loosed.
So let him hurl his smoky lightning flame,
and throw into turmoil all things in the world,
with white-winged snowflakes and deep bellowing
thunder beneath the earth: he shall not bend me   995
by all of this to tell him who is fated
to drive him from his tyranny.

HERMES

Think, here and now, if this seems to your interest.

PROMETHEUS

I have already thought—and laid my plans.

HERMES

Bring your proud heart to recognize discretion—
O foolish spirit—in the face of ruin.   1000

PROMETHEUS

You're annoying me pointlessly, as if you were
advising the waves. Let it not cross your mind
that any fear of Zeus will make me turn
womanish-minded, or that I shall entreat
the one I hate so greatly, with prayerful hands,   1005
to loose me from my chains: I am far from that.

HERMES

I have said too much already—so I think—
and said it all in vain: you are not softened;
your purpose is not dented by my prayers.
You're like a colt new-broken, with the bit   1010
clenched in its teeth, fighting against the reins,
and bolting. You are far too bold and confident

in your weak cleverness. For obstinacy
standing alone is the weakest of all things
in one whose mind is not possessed by wisdom.
Think what a storm, what triple wave of ruin   1015
will rise against you, if you will not hear me,
and there's no escape for you. First this rough crag
with thunder and the lightning bolt the Father
shall split in pieces, and shall hide your body
wrapped in a rocky clasp within its depth;
a vast extent of time you must fulfill   1020
before you see the light again, returning.
Then Zeus's winged hound, the blood-red eagle,
shall butcher tatters of your flesh, a feaster
coming unbidden, every day: your liver
bloodied to blackness will be his repast.   1025
And of this pain do not expect an end
until some god shall show himself successor
to take your tortures for himself, agreeing
to go down to lightless Hades and the shadows
of Tartarus' depths. Bear all this in mind
and so determine. This is no feigned boast   1030
but all too surely spoken. The mouth of Zeus
does not know how to lie, but every word
he brings to fulfilment. Look, you, and reflect
and never think that obstinacy is better
than wise counsel.   1035

CHORUS LEADER
             Hermes seems to us
to speak not altogether out of season.
He bids you quit your obstinacy and seek
a wise good counsel. Listen to him. Shame
it were for one so wise to fall in error.

PROMETHEUS [*chanting*]
Before he told it I knew this message,   1040
and there is no disgrace in suffering

at an enemy's hand, when the hate is mutual.
So, let the curling tendril of fire
from the lightning bolt be sent against me;
let the air be stirred with thunderclaps,   1045
winds with their blasts convulse the world;
let earth be shaken to her foundations,
roots and all, by the blasts of the storm;
let the waves of the sea confuse the paths
of heavenly stars in a fierce torrent;   1050
this body of mine, let him hurl it to hell,
to the blackness of Tartarus, with harsh eddies
of fierce necessity! But he shall never
bring me to death.

HERMES [*chanting*]
Such words are a madman's, a lunatic's plan:
every note's out of tune in his boastful song;   1055
his mind is deranged.
          But you now, at least,
you, who are so sympathetic with his troubles,
get away from this place, quickly go elsewhere,   1060
lest the hard and deafening roar of the thunder
destroy your wits.

CHORUS [*chanting*]
          No, say something else
different from this: give me other advice
that might persuade me; this word of yours
was intolerable, that you lured me with.   1065
How can you tell us to act like cowards?
I want to endure along with him
what we must endure.
I have learned to hate all traitors; no
disease do I spit on more than treachery.   1070

HERMES [*chanting*]
Well, remember my warning before it happens:
when you are overtaken by ruin don't then

blame fortune—don't say that it was Zeus
that brought you to calamity
quite unforeseen. Do not do this,   1075
but blame yourselves; for now you know
what you are doing, so neither suddenly
nor secretly your own lack of good sense
will have tangled you all in the net of ruin,
past all hope of rescue.

(Exit Hermes to the side. Sounds of thunder and lightning are heard.)°

PROMETHEUS [chanting]
Now it's words no longer: now in truth   1080
the earth is staggered; in its depths the thunder
bellows and roars, the fiery tendrils
of the lightning-flash blaze out, and clouds
carry the dust along in whirls.
All the winds' blasts   1085
dance in a fury one against the other
in violent confusion: sky and sea
are one, all mingled together.
Such is the storm
that comes against me plainly from Zeus   1090
to work its terrors. O holy Mother,
O sky that circling brings light to all,
you see how unjustly I suffer!

(Exit.)

OEDIPUS THE KING

SOPHOCLES
Translated by David Grene

INTRODUCTION TO SOPHOCLES' OEDIPUS THE KING

The date is unknown. Many scholars are inclined to place it about 427 BCE, shortly after the great plague at Athens, which they think may have suggested the plague at Thebes in the play. But there is no reliable evidence. We happen to be told that this play, on its first presentation, gained Sophocles only the second prize.

Aeschylus had already composed a Theban trilogy, of which an *Oedipus* (lost) was the second play, and we may assume that the largest outlines of the story were familiar to all. Or at least so much: that it was predicted that Oedipus would kill his father and marry his mother; that, unwittingly, he did both; and that these offenses were discovered and made public. Concerning details, there were certainly variations. There were different stories about how, when, and where Oedipus died; Euripides in his lost *Oedipus* had the hero blinded by the henchmen of Laius; the traditions about Antigone and Ismene are not fixed.

Still, in *Oedipus the King*, once the hero appears and announces his identity, the audience will know the great glaring facts about Oedipus and will realize almost at once that Oedipus does not know these facts. The situation makes for a story heavily charged with irony. The advance of the action consists of a probing into the past. Every "act" or episode brings in a new "helper"— Oedipus himself, Creon, Teiresias, Jocasta, Messenger, Herdsman—each of whom contributes his clue, until the whole secret is out. A fresh dimension of irony lies in the fact that the ghastly tragedy is mounted on the frame of a happy romance—the lost baby miraculously saved, thought dead but restored and united with his parents. The search for the murderer of Laius and the identity of Oedipus come out at the same point. The discovery is the climax.

Some have wanted to interpret *Oedipus the King* as a story of the punishment of pride, overconfidence, and hot temper. But such an interpretation is only of limited value. The deeds for which this hero would be "punished" were preordained before he was even conceived. Yet it is true that the endowments which make him grand—his impulsive intellect, his passion for truth, his integrity, and his pride—all contribute to the pattern of his fate, down to its final fulfillment in the realization of what that fate has been.

OEDIPUS THE KING

Characters   OEDIPUS, king of Thebes
                A PRIEST
                CREON, his brother-in-law (Jocasta's brother)
                CHORUS of old men of Thebes
                TEIRESIAS, an old blind prophet
                JOCASTA, his wife (and mother)
                FIRST MESSENGER
                A HERDSMAN
                SECOND MESSENGER

Scene: In front of the palace of Oedipus at Thebes. On one side stands the Priest with a crowd of children.

                        (Enter Oedipus, from the palace door.)

OEDIPUS

    Children, young sons and daughters of old Cadmus,
    why do you sit here with your suppliant crowns?
    The town is heavy with a mingled burden
    of sounds and smells, of groans and hymns and incense;   5
    I did not think it fit that I should hear
    of this from messengers but came myself—
    I, Oedipus whom all men call the Great.

                          (To the Priest.)

    You're old and they are young; come, speak for them.
    What do you fear or want, that you sit here   10
    suppliant? Indeed I'm willing to give all

that you may need; I would be very hard
should I not pity suppliants like these.

PRIEST
   O ruler of my country, Oedipus,
you see our company around the altar;   15
you see our ages; some of us, like these,
who cannot yet fly far, and some of us
heavy with age; these children are the chosen
among the young, and I the priest of Zeus.
Within the market place sit others crowned   20
with suppliant garlands, at the double shrine
of Pallas and the temple where Ismenus
gives oracles by fire. King, you yourself
have seen our city reeling like a wreck
already; it can scarcely lift its prow
out of the depths, out of the bloody surf.
A blight is on the fruitful plants of the earth,   25
a blight is on the cattle in the fields,
a blight is on our women that no children
are born to them; a god that carries fire,
a deadly pestilence, is on our town,
strikes us and spares not, and the house of Cadmus
is emptied of its people while black Death
grows rich in groaning and in lamentation.   30
     We have not come as suppliants to this altar
because we think of you as of a god,
but rather judging you the first of men
in all the chances of this life and when
we mortals have to do with more than man.
You came and by your coming saved our city,   35
freed us from tribute which we paid of old
to the Sphinx, cruel singer. This you did
in virtue of no knowledge we could give you,
in virtue of no teaching; it was god
that aided you, men say, and you are held

with god's assistance to have saved our lives.
     Now Oedipus, greatest in all men's eyes,   40
here falling at your feet we all entreat you,
find us some strength for rescue.
Perhaps you'll hear a wise word from some god,
perhaps you will learn something from a man
(for I have seen that for those with experience
the outcomes of their counsels live the most).   45
Noblest of men, go, and raise up our city,
go—and give heed. For now this land of ours
calls you its savior since you saved it once.
So, let us never speak about your reign
as of a time when first our feet were set   50
secure and straight, but later fell to ruin.
Raise up our city, save it and set it straight.
Once you have brought us luck with happy omen;
be no less now in fortune.
If you will rule this land, as now you rule it,
better to rule it full of men than empty.   55
For neither tower nor ship is anything
when empty, and none live in it together.

OEDIPUS

I pity you, children. You have come full of longing,
but I have known the story before you told it
only too well. I know you are all sick,   60
yet there is not one of you, sick though you are,
that is as sick as I myself.
Your several sorrows each have single scope
and touch but one of you. My spirit groans
for city and myself and you at once.
You have not roused me like a man from sleep;   65
know that I have given many tears to this,
gone many ways wandering in thought.
But as I thought I found only one remedy
and that I took. I sent Menoeceus' son

Creon, Jocasta's brother, to Apollo,
to his Pythian temple,   70
that he might learn there by what act or word
I could save this city. As I count the days,
it worries me what he's doing; he is gone
far longer than he needed for the journey.   75
But when he comes, then, may I prove a villain,
if I shall not do all the god commands.

PRIEST
    Your words are opportune: for here, your men
    signal that Creon is this moment coming.

OEDIPUS
    O holy lord Apollo, may his news   80
    be bright for us and bring us light and safety.°

PRIEST
    It is happy news, I think, for else his head
    would not be crowned with sprigs of fruitful laurel.

                    (Enter Creon, from one side.)

OEDIPUS
    We will know soon,
    he's within hail. Lord Creon, my good kinsman,   85
    what is the word you bring us from the god?

CREON
    A good word—for even things quite hard to bear,
    if the final issue turns out well,
    I count complete good fortune.

OEDIPUS
    What do you mean? What you have said so far
    leaves me uncertain whether to trust or fear.   90

CREON
    If you'll hear my news in the presence of these others
    I am ready to speak, or else to go within.

OEDIPUS

Speak it to all; the grief I bear, I bear it
more for these people than for my own life.

CREON

I will tell you, then, what I heard from the god.   95
King Phoebus in plain words commanded us
to drive out a pollution from our land,
pollution grown ingrained within the soil;
drive it out, said the god, not cherish it,
till it's past cure.

OEDIPUS

                    What is the rite
of purification? How shall it be done?

CREON

By banishing a man, or expiation   100
of blood by blood, since it is murder guilt
which shakes our city in this destroying storm.

OEDIPUS

Who is this man whose fate the god pronounces?

CREON

My Lord, before you piloted the state
we had a king called Laius.

OEDIPUS

I know of him by hearsay. I never saw him.   105

CREON

The god commanded clearly: that we must
punish with force this dead man's murderers,
whoever they are.

OEDIPUS

Where are they in the world? Where would a trace
of this old crime be found? It would be hard
to guess where.

CREON

    The guilt is in this land;   110

    that which is sought can be found;

    the unheeded thing escapes:

    so said the god.

OEDIPUS

    Was it at home, or in the countryside

    that death came to Laius, or traveling abroad?

CREON

    He left, he said himself, upon an embassy,

    but never returned after he set out from home.   115

OEDIPUS

    Was there no messenger, no fellow traveler

    who saw what happened? Such a one might tell

    something of use.

CREON

    They were all killed save one. He fled in terror

    and he could tell us nothing in clear terms

    of what he knew, except for one thing only.

OEDIPUS

    What was it?

    If we could even find a slim beginning   120

    in which to hope, we might discover much.

CREON

    This man said that the robbers they encountered

    were many and the hands that did the murder

    were many; it was no man's single power.

OEDIPUS

    How could a robber dare a deed like this

    were he not helped with money from the city?   125

CREON

    That indeed was thought. But Laius was dead

    and in our trouble there was none to help.

OEDIPUS

What trouble was so great to hinder you
inquiring out the murder of your king?

CREON

The riddling Sphinx induced us to neglect   130
mysterious crimes and rather seek solution
of troubles at our feet.

OEDIPUS

I'll begin again and bring this all to light.
Fittingly King Phoebus took this care
about the dead, and you too, fittingly.
And justly you will see in me an ally,   135
a champion of this country and the god.
For when I drive pollution from the land
I will not serve a distant friend's advantage,
but act in my own interest. Whoever
he was that killed the king may readily
wish to dispatch me with his murderous hand;   140
so helping the dead king I help myself.
         Come, children, take your suppliant boughs and go;
up from the altars now. Call the assembly
and let the people of Cadmus meet and know
that I'll do everything. God will decide   145
whether we shall prosper or shall fail.

PRIEST

Rise, children—it was this we came to seek,
which of himself the king now offers us.
May Phoebus who gave us the oracle
come to our rescue and stop the plague.   150

(Exit all. The Chorus enters from the side.)

CHORUS [*singing*]

STROPHE A

What is the sweet spoken word of god from the shrine of Pytho
rich in gold

that has come to glorious Thebes?
I am stretched on the rack of doubt, and terror and trembling hold
my heart, O Delian Healer, and I worship full of fears   155
for what doom you will bring to pass, new or renewed in the
revolving years.
Speak to me, immortal voice,
child of golden Hope.

First I call on you, Athena, deathless daughter of Zeus,
and Artemis, Earth upholder,   160
who sits in the midst of the marketplace in the throne which
men call Fame,
and Phoebus, the far-shooter, three averters of Fate,
come to us now, if ever before, when ruin rushed upon the state,   165
you drove destruction's flame away
out of our land.

Our sorrows defy number;
all the ship's timbers are rotten;
taking of thought is no spear for the driving away of the plague.   170
There are no growing children in this famous land;
there are no women bearing the pangs of childbirth.
You may see them one with another, like birds swift on the wing,   175
quicker than fire unmastered,
speeding away to the coast of the Western god.

In the unnumbered deaths
of its people the city dies;   180
the children that are born lie dead on the naked earth
unpitied, spreading contagion of death; and grey-haired mothers
and wives
everywhere stand at the altar's edge, suppliant, moaning;   185
the hymn to the healing god rings out, but with it the wailing
voices are blended.

From these our sufferings grant us, O golden Daughter of Zeus,
glad-faced deliverance.

There is no clash of brazen shields but our fight is with the war god,   190
a war god ringed with the cries of men, a savage god who burns us;
grant that he turn in racing course backward out of our country's
    bounds
to the great palace of Amphitrite or where the waves of the
    Thracian sea   195
deny the stranger safe anchorage.
Whatsoever escapes the night
at last the light of day revisits;°
so smite him, Father Zeus,
beneath your thunderbolt,   200
for you are the lord of the lightning, the lightning that carries fire.

ANTISTROPHE C

And your unconquered arrow shafts, winged by the
    golden-corded bow,
Lycian king, I beg to be at our side for help;
and the gleaming torches of Artemis with which she scours the
Lycian hills,   205
and I call on the god with the turban of gold, who gave his name
to this country of ours,   210
the Bacchic god with the wind-flushed face,
you who travel with the maenad company crying Euhoi,
come with your torch of pine;
for the god that is our enemy is a god unhonored among the gods.   215

(Enter Oedipus.)

OEDIPUS

For what you ask me—if you will hear my words,
and hearing welcome them and fight the plague,
you will find strength and lightening of your load.
Listen now to me; what I say to you, I say
as one that is a stranger to the story   220

[125] OEDIPUS THE KING

as stranger to the deed. For I would not
be far upon the track if I alone
were tracing it without a clue or helper.
But since, though late, I also have become
a citizen among you, citizens—
now I proclaim to all the men of Thebes:
who so among you knows the murderer
by whose hand Laius, son of Labdacus,   225
died—I command him to tell everything
to me—yes, though he fears himself to take the blame
on his own head; for bitter punishment
he shall have none, but leave this land unharmed.
Or if he knows the murderer, another,   230
maybe a foreigner, still let him speak the truth.
For I will pay him and be grateful, too.
But if you shall keep silence, if perhaps
some one of you, to shield a guilty friend,
or for his own sake shall reject my words—
hear what I shall do then: 235
I forbid that man, whoever he be, my land,
this land where I hold sovereignty and throne;
and I forbid any to welcome him
or give him greeting or make him a sharer
in sacrifice or offering to the gods,
or give him water for his hands to wash.   240
I command all to drive him from their homes,
since he is our pollution, as the oracle
of Pytho's god proclaimed him now to me.
So I stand forth a champion of the god
and of the man who died.   245
Upon the murderer I invoke this curse—°
whether he is one man and all unknown,
or one of many—may he wear out his life
in misery to miserable doom!
If with my knowledge he lives at my hearth   250
I pray that I myself may feel my curse.

On you I lay my charge to fulfill all this
for me, for the god, and for this land of ours
destroyed and blighted, by the gods forsaken.
Even were this no matter of god's ordinance   255
it did not fit you so to leave it lie,
unpurified, since a great man is dead,
a king. Indeed, you should have searched it out.
Since I am now the holder of his office,
and have his bed and wife that once was his,   260
and had his line not been unfortunate
we would have children in common—(but fortune leaped
upon his head)—because of all these things,
I fight in his defense as for my father,   265
and I shall try all means to take the murderer
of Laius the son of Labdacus
the son of Polydorus and before him
of Cadmus and before him of Agenor.

    Those who do not obey me, may the gods
grant no crops springing from the ground they plough   270
nor children to their women! May a fate
like this, or one still worse than this, consume them!
For you whom these words please, the other Thebans,
may Justice as your ally and all the gods
live with you, blessing you now and for ever!   275

CHORUS LEADER

As you have held me to my oath, I speak:
I neither killed the king nor can declare
the killer; but since Phoebus set the quest
it is his part to tell us who has done it.

OEDIPUS

Right; but to put compulsion on the gods   280
against their will—no man can do that.

CHORUS LEADER

May I then say what I think second best?

OEDIPUS

If there's a third best, too, spare not to tell it.

CHORUS LEADER

I know that what the lord Teiresias
sees is most often what the lord Apollo   285
sees. If you should inquire of this from him
you might find out most clearly.

OEDIPUS

Even in this my actions have not been slow.
On Creon's word I have sent two messengers,
and why the prophet is not here already
I have been wondering.

CHORUS LEADER

                                His skill apart,
there is besides only an old faint story.   290

OEDIPUS

What is it? I look at every rumor.

CHORUS LEADER

It was said that he was killed by certain wayfarers.

OEDIPUS

I heard that, too, but no one sees who did it.°

CHORUS LEADER

Yet if he has a share of fear at all,
his courage will not stand firm, hearing your curse.   295

OEDIPUS

The man who in the doing did not shrink
will fear no word.

CHORUS LEADER

     Here comes his prosecutor:
led by these men the godly prophet comes,
in whom alone of humankind the truth
is his by nature.

(Enter Teiresias from the side, led by a boy.)

OEDIPUS

Teiresias, you are versed in everything,   300
things teachable and things not to be spoken,
things of the heaven and earth-creeping things.
You have no eyes but in your mind you know
with what a plague our city is afflicted.
My lord, in you alone we find a champion,
in you alone one that can rescue us.
Perhaps you have not heard the messengers,   305
but Phoebus sent in answer to our sending
an oracle declaring that our freedom
from this disease would only come when we
should learn the names of those who killed King Laius,
and kill them or expel from our country.
Do not begrudge us messages from birds,   310
or any other way of prophecy
within your skill; save yourself and the city,
save me; save all of us from this pollution
that lies on us because of that dead man.
We are in your hands; it's a man's most noble labor
to help another when he has the means and power.   315

TEIRESIAS

Alas, how terrible is wisdom when
it brings no profit to the man that's wise!
This I knew well, but had forgotten it,
else I would not have come here.

OEDIPUS

        What is this?
How gloomy you are now you've come!

TEIRESIAS

                  Let me
go home. It will be easiest for us both   320

to bear our several destinies to the end
if you will follow my advice.

OEDIPUS
                    You'd rob us
of this your gift of prophecy? You talk
as one who had no care for law nor love
for Thebes who reared you.

TEIRESIAS
Yes, but I see that even your own words
miss the mark; therefore I must fear for mine.   325

OEDIPUS
For god's sake if you know of anything,
do not turn from us; all of us kneel to you,
all of us here, your suppliants.

TEIRESIAS
All of you here know nothing. I will not
bring to the light of day my troubles, mine—
rather than call them yours.

OEDIPUS
                    What do you mean?
You know of something but refuse to speak.   330
Would you betray us and destroy the city?

TEIRESIAS
I will not bring this pain upon us both,
neither on you nor on myself. Why is it
you question me and waste your labor? I
will tell you nothing.

OEDIPUS
You would provoke a stone! Tell us, you villain,
tell us, and do not stand there quietly   335
unmoved, unhelpful, set on doing nothing.

TEIRESIAS

    You blame my temper but you do not see
    your own that lives within you; so you chide
    me instead.

OEDIPUS

    Who would not feel his temper rise
    at words like these with which you shame our city?   340

TEIRESIAS

    Of themselves things will come, although I hide them
    and breathe no word of them.

OEDIPUS

            Since they will come
    tell them to me.

TEIRESIAS

            I will say nothing further.
    Against this answer let your temper rage
    as wildly as you will.

OEDIPUS

           Indeed I am
    so angry I shall not hold back a jot   345
    of what I think. For I would have you know
    I think you were coplotter of the deed
    and doer of the deed save insofar
    as for the actual killing. Had you had eyes
    I would have said alone you murdered him.

TEIRESIAS

    Yes? Then I warn you faithfully to keep   350
    the letter of your proclamation and
    from this day forth to speak no word of greeting
    to these nor me; you are the land's pollution.

OEDIPUS

    How shamelessly you started up this taunt!
    How do you think you will escape?   355

TEIRESIAS

        I have.
I have escaped; the truth is what I cherish
and that's my strength.

OEDIPUS

        And who has taught you truth?
Not your profession surely!

TEIRESIAS

        You have taught me,
for you have made me speak against my will.

OEDIPUS

Speak what? Tell me again that I may learn it better.

TEIRESIAS

Did you not understand before or would you   360
provoke me into speaking?

OEDIPUS

        I did not grasp it,
not so to call it known. Say it again.

TEIRESIAS

I say you are the murderer of the king
whose murderer you seek.

OEDIPUS

        Not twice you shall
say ghastly things like this and stay unpunished.

TEIRESIAS

Shall I say more to tempt your anger further?

OEDIPUS

As much as you wish; it will be said in vain.   365

TEIRESIAS

I say that, unknowing, with those you love the best

you live in foulest shame unconsciously
and do not see where you are in calamity.

OEDIPUS

Do you imagine you can always talk
like this, and live to rejoice at it hereafter?

TEIRESIAS

Yes, if the truth has anything of strength.

OEDIPUS

It has, but not for you; it has no strength   370
for you because you are blind in mind and ears
as well as in your eyes.

TEIRESIAS

                    You are a poor wretch
to taunt me with the very insults which
everyone soon will heap upon yourself.

OEDIPUS

Your life is one long night so that you cannot
hurt me or any other who sees the light.   375

TEIRESIAS

It is not fate that I should be your ruin,
Apollo is enough; it is his care
to work this out.

OEDIPUS

                    Was this your own design
or Creon's?

TEIRESIAS

                    Creon is no hurt to you.
but you are to yourself.

OEDIPUS

Wealth, kingly rule, and skill outmatching skill   380

for the contrivance of an envied life!
How great a store of jealousy you are hoarding,
if, for the sake of the office which I hold,
given me by the city, not sought by me,
my friend Creon, friend from the first and loyal,   385
thus secretly attacks me, secretly
desires to drive me out and secretly
suborns this juggling, trick-devising quack,
this wily beggar who has only eyes
for his own gains, but blindness in his skill.

　　　For, tell me, where have you seen clear, Teiresias,   390
with your prophetic mind? When the dark singer,
the Sphinx, was in your country, did you speak
word of deliverance to these citizens?
Yet solving the riddle then was not the province
of a chance comer: it was a prophet's task,
and plainly you had no such gift of prophecy
from birds nor otherwise from any god   395
to glean a word of knowledge. But I came,
Oedipus, who knew nothing, and I stopped her.
I solved the riddle by my wit alone.
Mine was no knowledge got from birds. And now
you would expel me,
because you think that you will find a place   400
by Creon's throne. I think you will be sorry,
both you and your accomplice, for your plot
to drive me out. And did I not regard you
as an old man, some suffering would have taught you
that what was in your heart was treason.

CHORUS LEADER
We look at this man's words and yours, my king,
and we find both have spoken them in anger.   405
We need no angry words but only thought
how we may best hit the god's meaning for us.

TEIRESIAS

    If you are king, at least I have the right
    no less to speak in my defense against you.
    Of that much I am master. I am no slave
    of yours, but Loxias', and so I shall not   410
    enroll myself with Creon for my patron.
    Since you have taunted me with being blind,
    here is my word for you.
    You have your eyes but see not where you are
    in evil, nor where you live, nor whom you live with.
    Do you know who your parents are? Unknowing   415
    you are an enemy to kith and kin
    in death, beneath the earth, and in this life.
    A deadly footed, double-striking curse,
    from father and mother both, shall drive you forth
    out of this land, with darkness on your eyes,
    that now have such straight vision. Shall there be
    a place will not be harbor to your cries,   420
    a corner of Cithaeron will not ring°
    in echo to your laments, soon, soon,
    when you shall learn the secret of your marriage,
    which steered you to a haven in this house,
    haven no haven, after lucky voyage?
    And of the multitude of other evils
    establishing a grim equality°   425
    between you and your children, you know nothing.
    So, muddy with contempt my words and Creon's!
    Misery shall grind no man as it will you.

OEDIPUS

    Is it endurable that I should hear
    such words from him? Go and a curse go with you!   430
    Quick, home with you! Away from my house at once!

TEIRESIAS

    I would not have come either, had you not called me.

OEDIPUS

    I did not know then you would talk like a fool—
    or it would have been long before I called you.

TEIRESIAS

    I am a fool then, as it seems to you—   435
    but to the parents who begot you, wise.

OEDIPUS

    What parents? Stop! Who are they of all the world?

TEIRESIAS

    This day will show your birth and will destroy you.

OEDIPUS

    How needlessly your riddles darken everything.

TEIRESIAS

    But aren't you best at answering such riddles?   440

OEDIPUS

    Yes. Taunt me where you will find me great.

TEIRESIAS

    It is this very luck that has destroyed you.

OEDIPUS

    I do not care, if it has saved this city.

TEIRESIAS

    Well, I will go. Come, boy, lead me away.

OEDIPUS

    Yes, lead him off. So long as you are here,   445
    you are a stumbling block and a vexation;
    once gone, you will not trouble me again.

TEIRESIAS

    I have said
    what I came here to say not fearing your
    countenance: there is no way you can hurt me.

I tell you, king, this man, this murderer   450
(whom you have long declared you are in search of,
indicting him in threatening proclamation
as murderer of Laius)—he is here.
In name he is a stranger among citizens
but soon he will be shown to be homegrown,
true native Theban, and he'll have no joy
of the discovery: blindness for sight
and beggary for riches his exchange,   455
he shall go journeying to a foreign country
tapping his way before him with a stick.
He shall be proved father and brother both
to his own children in his house; to her
that gave him birth, a son and husband both;
a fellow sower in his father's bed
with that same father that he murdered.   460
Go within, reckon that out, and if you find me
mistaken, say I have no skill in prophecy.

(Exit separately, Teiresias to the side, Oedipus indoors.)

CHORUS [*singing*]

STROPHE A

Who is the man proclaimed
by Delphi's prophetic rock
as the bloody-handed murderer,   465
the doer of deeds that none dare name?
Now is the time for him to run
with a stronger foot
than wind-swift Pegasus
for the child of Zeus leaps in arms upon him   470
with fire and the lightning bolt,
and terribly close on his heels
are the Fates that never miss.

ANTISTROPHE A

Lately from snowy Parnassus
clearly the voice flashed forth,

bidding everyone track him down,   475
the unknown murderer.
In the savage forests he lurks and in
the caverns like
the mountain bull.
He is sad and lonely, and lonely his feet°
that carry him far from the navel of earth;   480
but its prophecies, ever living,
flutter around his head.

STROPHE B

The skilled bird-prophet bewilders me terribly;
I do not approve what was said
nor can I deny it.   485
I do not know what to say;
I am in a flutter of foreboding;
I do not see the present
nor the past; I never heard of a quarrel between
the sons of Labdacus and of Polybus,
neither in the past nor now,   490
that I might bring as proof
in attacking the popular fame
of Oedipus, seeking   495
to take vengeance for undiscovered
death in the line of Labdacus.

ANTISTROPHE B

Truly Zeus and Apollo are wise
and in human things all-knowing;
but amongst men there is no
distinct judgment, between the prophet
and me—which of us is right.   500
One man may pass another in wisdom
but I would never agree
with those that find fault with the king
till I should see the word   505
proved right beyond doubt. For once

in visible form the Sphinx
came against him, and all of us
saw his wisdom and in that test 510
he saved the city. So he will not be condemned by my mind.

(Enter Creon, from the side.)

CREON

Citizens, I have come because I heard
deadly words spread about me, that the king
accuses me. I cannot take that from him. 515
If he believes that in these present troubles
he has been wronged by me in word or deed
I do not want to live on with the burden
of such a scandal on me. The report
injures me doubly and most vitally— 520
for I'll be called a traitor to my city
and traitor also to my friends and you.

CHORUS LEADER

Perhaps it was a sudden gust of anger
that forced that insult from him, and no judgment.

CREON

But did he say that it was in compliance 525
with schemes of mine that the seer told him lies?

CHORUS LEADER

Yes, he said that, but why, I do not know.

CREON

Were his eyes straight in his head? Was his mind right
when he accused me in this fashion?

CHORUS LEADER

I do not know; I have no eyes to see 530
what princes do. Here comes the king himself.

(Enter Oedipus, from the palace.)

OEDIPUS

You, sir, how is it you come here? Have you so much
brazen-faced daring that you venture to
my house although you are proved manifestly
the murderer of that man, and though you tried,
openly, highway robbery of my crown?   535
For god's sake, tell me what you saw in me,
what cowardice or what stupidity,
that made you lay a plot like this against me?
Did you imagine I should not observe
your crafty scheme that stole upon me or
seeing it, take no means to counter it?
Was it not stupid of you to make the attempt,   540
to try to hunt down royal power without
the people at your back or friends? For only
with the people at your back and money can
this hunt end in the capture of a crown.

CREON

Do you know what you're doing? Will you listen
to words to answer yours, and then pass judgment?

OEDIPUS

You're quick to speak, but I am slow to grasp you,   545
for I have found you dangerous—and my foe.

CREON

First of all hear what I shall say to that.

OEDIPUS

At least don't tell me that you are not guilty.

CREON

If you think obstinacy without wisdom
a valuable possession, you are wrong.   550

OEDIPUS

And you are wrong if you believe that one
can harm a kinsman and then not be punished.

CREON

    This is but just—
    but tell me, then, of what offense I'm guilty.

OEDIPUS

    Did you or did you not urge me to send   555
    to this prophetic mumbler?

CREON

    I did indeed,
    and I shall stand by what I told you.

OEDIPUS

    How long ago is it since Laius . . .

CREON

    What about Laius? I don't understand.

OEDIPUS

    Vanished—died—was murdered?   560

CREON

                 It is long,
    a long, long time to reckon.

OEDIPUS

               Was this prophet
    in the profession then?

CREON

             He was, and honored
    as highly as he is today.

OEDIPUS

    At that time did he say a word about me?

CREON

    Never, at least when I was near him.   565

OEDIPUS

    You never made a search for the killer?°

CREON

   We searched, indeed, but never learned of anything.

OEDIPUS

   Why did our wise old friend not say this then?

CREON

   I don't know; and when I know nothing, I
   usually hold my tongue.

OEDIPUS

                     You know this much,   570
   and can declare it if you are truly loyal.

CREON

   What is it? If I know, I'll not deny it.

OEDIPUS

   That he would not have said that I killed Laius
   had he not met with you first.

CREON

                     You know yourself
   whether he said this, but I demand that I
   should hear as much from you as you from me.   575

OEDIPUS

   Then hear—I'll not be proved a murderer.

CREON

   Well, then. You're married to my sister?

OEDIPUS

                     Yes,
   that I am not disposed to deny.

CREON

                     You rule
   this country giving her an equal share
   in the government?

OEDIPUS

Yes, everything she wants
she has from me.   580

CREON

And I, as third with you,
am rated as the equal of you both?

OEDIPUS

Yes, and it's there you've proved yourself false friend.

CREON

Not if you will reflect on it as I do.
Consider, first, if you think anyone
would choose to rule and fear rather than rule   585
and sleep peacefully, if the power
were equal in both cases. I, at least,
I was not born with such a frantic yearning
to be a king—but to do what kings do.
And so it is with everyone who has learned
wisdom and self-control. As it stands now,   590
I get from you all the prizes—and without fear.
But if I were the king myself, I must
do much that went against the grain.
How should despotic rule seem sweeter to me
than painless power and an assured authority?
I am not so deluded yet that I
want other honors than those that come with profit.   595
Now all men wish me joy; every man greets me;
those who want things from you all fawn on me,
success for them depends upon my favor.
Why should I let all this go to win that?
My mind would not be traitor if it's wise;°   600
I am no treason lover, by my nature,
nor could I ever bear to join a plot.

Prove what I say. Go to the oracle

at Pytho and inquire about the answers,
if they are as I told you. For the rest,
if you discover I laid any plot 605
together with the seer, kill me, I say,
not only by your vote but by my own.
But do not charge me on obscure opinion
without some proof to back it. It's not just
lightly to count bad men as honest ones, 610
nor honest men as bad. To throw away
an honest friend is, as it were, to throw
your life away, which a man loves the best.
In time you'll know all this with certainty;
time is the only test of honest men,
one day is space enough to know who's bad. 615

CHORUS LEADER
His words are wise, king, for one who fears to fall.
Those who are quick of temper are not safe.

OEDIPUS
When he that plots against me secretly
moves quickly, I must quickly counterplot.
If I wait taking no decisive measure 620
his business will be done, and mine be spoiled.

CREON
What do you want to do then? Banish me?

OEDIPUS
No, certainly; kill you, not banish you.

CREON
I do not understand why you resent me so.°

. . . .

OEDIPUS
You speak as if you'll not listen nor obey. 625

CREON
I do not think that you've your wits about you.

OEDIPUS

For my own interests, yes.

CREON

But for mine, too,
you should think equally.

OEDIPUS

You are a traitor.

CREON

Suppose you do not understand?

OEDIPUS

But yet
I must be ruler.

CREON

Not if you rule badly.

OEDIPUS

O, city, city!

CREON

I too have some share   630
in the city; it is not yours alone.

CHORUS LEADER

Stop, my lords! Here—and in the nick of time
I see Jocasta coming from the house;
with her help settle the quarrel that now stirs you.

(Enter Jocasta, from the palace.)

JOCASTA

For shame! Why have you raised this foolish squabbling?
Are you not ashamed to air your private   635
troubles when the country's sick? Go inside, Oedipus,
and you, too, Creon, go to your house. Don't magnify
your nothing troubles.

CREON

      My sister: Oedipus,
your husband, thinks he has the right to do
terrible wrongs to me—he is choosing 640
between either banishing or killing me.°

OEDIPUS

He's right, Jocasta; for I find him plotting
with evil tricks against my person.

CREON

May never god bless me! May I die
accursed, if I've been guilty in any way
of any of the charges you bring against me! 645

JOCASTA

I beg you, Oedipus, trust him in this,
spare him for the sake of his oath to god,
for my sake, and the sake of those who stand here.

CHORUS [*singing in what follows, while Oedipus speaks*]

STROPHE

Think carefully: be gracious, be merciful,
we beg of you. 650

OEDIPUS

In what would you have me yield?

CHORUS

He has never been foolish in the past.
He is strong in his oath now.
Spare him.

OEDIPUS

Do you know what you ask?

CHORUS

Yes.

OEDIPUS

Tell me then. 655

CHORUS

He has been your friend, he has sworn an oath; do not cast him
away dishonored on an obscure conjecture.

OEDIPUS

I would have you know that this request of yours
really requests my death or banishment.

CHORUS

May the sun god, king of gods, forbid!   660
May I die without god's blessing, without friends' help,
if I had any such thought.
But my spirit is broken by my unhappiness for my wasting country;   665
and this would but add troubles amongst ourselves to the other
    troubles.

OEDIPUS

Well, let him go then—if I must die ten times for it,
or be sent out dishonored into exile.   670
It is your lips praying for him I pitied,
not his; wherever he is, I shall hate him.

CREON

I see you sulk in yielding and you're dangerous
when you are out of temper; natures like yours
are justly hardest for themselves to bear.   675

OEDIPUS

Leave me alone! Take yourself off, I tell you.

CREON

I'll go. You have not known me, but they have,
and they have known my innocence.

(Exit Creon, to the side.)

CHORUS [*singing in what follows, while Jocasta and Oedipus speak*]
               ANTISTROPHE
Won't you take him inside, lady?

JOCASTA

Yes, when I've found out what was the matter.   680

CHORUS

There was some misconceived suspicion
of a story, and on the other side
the sting of injustice.

JOCASTA

So, on both sides?

CHORUS

Yes.

JOCASTA

What was the story?

CHORUS

I think it best, in the interests of our country,   685
to leave it where it ended.

OEDIPUS

You see where you have ended, straight of judgment
although you are, by softening my anger.

CHORUS

Sir, I have said before and I say again—   690
be sure that I would have been proved a madman,
bankrupt in sane council,
if I should put you away, you who steered the country I love safely
when it was crazed with troubles. God grant that now, too,   695
you may prove a fortunate guide for us.

JOCASTA

Tell me, my lord, I beg of you, what was it
that roused your anger so?

OEDIPUS

                 Yes, I will tell you.   700
I honor you more than I honor them.
It was Creon and the plots he laid against me.

JOCASTA

Tell me—if you can clearly tell the quarrel—

OEDIPUS

Creon says that I'm the murderer of Laius.

JOCASTA

Of his own knowledge or on information?

OEDIPUS

He sent this rascal prophet to me, since   705
he keeps his own mouth clean of any guilt.

JOCASTA

Do not concern yourself about this matter;
listen to me and learn that human beings
have no part in the craft of prophecy.
Of that I'll show you a short proof.   710
There was an oracle once that came to Laius—
I will not say that it was Phoebus' own,
but it was from his servants—and it told him
that it was fate that he should die a victim
at the hands of his own son, a son to be born
of Laius and me. But, see now, he,
the king, was killed by foreign highway robbers   715
at a place where three roads meet—so goes the story;
and for the son—before three days were out
after his birth King Laius pierced his ankles
and by the hands of others cast him forth
upon a pathless hillside. So Apollo
failed to fulfill his oracle to the son,   720
that he should kill his father, and to Laius
also proved false in that the thing he feared,
death at his son's hands, never came to pass.
So clear in this case were the oracles,
describing the future. Give them no heed, I say;
what the god discovers need of, easily
he will show to us himself.   725

OEDIPUS

O dear Jocasta,
as I hear this from you, what wandering in my soul
now comes upon me—what turbulence of mind.

JOCASTA

What trouble is it, that you turn again
and speak like this?

OEDIPUS

I thought I heard you say
that Laius was killed at a crossroads.   730

JOCASTA

Yes, that was how the story went and still
that word goes round.

OEDIPUS

Where is this place, Jocasta,
where he was murdered?

JOCASTA

Phocis is the country
and the road splits there, one of two roads from Delphi,
another comes from Daulia.

OEDIPUS

How long ago was this?   735

JOCASTA

The news came to the city just before
you became king and all men's eyes looked to you.
What is it, Oedipus, that's in your mind?

OEDIPUS

What have you designed, O Zeus, to do with me?

JOCASTA

What is the thought that troubles your heart?

OEDIPUS

Don't ask me yet—tell me of Laius— 740
How did he look? How old or young was he?

JOCASTA

He was a tall man and his hair was grizzled
already—partly white—and in his form
not unlike you.

OEDIPUS

O god, I think I have
called curses on myself in ignorance. 745

JOCASTA

What do you mean? I'm frightened now, my king,
when I look at you.

OEDIPUS

I have a deadly fear
that the old seer had eyes. You'll show me more
if you can tell me one more thing.

JOCASTA

I will.
I'm frightened—but you ask and I will listen,
I'll tell you all I know.

OEDIPUS

How was his company? 750
Had he few with him when he went this journey,
or many servants, as would suit a prince?

JOCASTA

In all there were but five, and among them
a herald; and one carriage for the king.

OEDIPUS

It's plain—it's plain—who was it told you this? 755

JOCASTA

The only servant that escaped safe home.

OEDIPUS

Is he at home now?

JOCASTA

No, when he came home again
and saw that you were king and Laius dead,
he came to me and touched my hand and begged   760
that I should send him to the fields to be
my shepherd and so he might see the city
as far off as he could. So I
sent him away. He was an honest man,
as slaves go, and was worthy of far more
than what he asked of me.

OEDIPUS

So could he quickly now be brought back here?   765

JOCASTA

It can be done. Why is your heart so set on this?

OEDIPUS

O dear Jocasta, I am full of fears
that I have spoken far too much; and therefore
I wish to see this shepherd.

JOCASTA

He will come;
but, Oedipus, I think I too deserve
to know what is it that disquiets you.   770

OEDIPUS

It shall not be kept from you, since my mind
has gone so far with its forebodings. Whom
should I confide in rather than you? Who is there
of more importance to me who have passed
through such a fortune?
Polybus was my father, king of Corinth,

and Merope, the Dorian, my mother. 775
I was held greatest of the citizens
in Corinth till a curious chance befell me,
as I shall tell you—curious, indeed,
but hardly worth the store I set upon it.
There was a dinner and at it was a man,
a drunken man, who accused me in his drink
of being bastard. I was furious 780
but held my temper under for that day.
Next day I went and taxed my parents with it;
they took the insult ill and came down hard
on the man who had uttered it. So I
was comforted with regard to the two of them; 785
but still this thing rankled with me, for the story
kept on recurring. And so I went at last
to Pytho, though my parents did not know.
But Phoebus sent me home again unhonored
in what I came to learn, but he foretold
other and desperate horrors to befall me, 790
that I was fated to lie with my mother,
and show to daylight an accursed breed
which men would not endure, and I was doomed
to be murderer of the father that begot me.

When I heard this I fled, and in the days
that followed I would measure from the stars 795
the whereabouts of Corinth—yes, I fled
to somewhere where I should not see fulfilled
the infamies told in that dreadful oracle.
And as I journeyed I came to the place
where, as you say, this king met with his death.
Jocasta, I will tell you the whole truth. 800
When I was near that branching of the crossroads,
going on foot, I was encountered by
a herald and a carriage with a man in it,
just as you tell me. He that led the way
and the old man himself wanted to thrust me 805

out of the road by force. I became angry
and struck the coachman who was pushing me.
When the old man saw this he waited for his chance,
and as I passed he struck me from his carriage,
full on the head with his two-pointed goad.
He paid for this in full, and more: my stick   810
quickly struck him backward from the car
and he rolled out of it. And then I killed them
all. If it happens there was any tie
of kinship between this man and Laius,
who is there now more miserable than I,   815
what man on earth so hated by the gods,
since neither citizen nor foreigner
may welcome me at home or even greet me,
but drive me out of doors? And it is I,
I and no other have so cursed myself.   820
And I pollute the bed of him I killed
by the hands that killed him. Was I not born evil?
Am I not utterly unclean, if I have to flee
and in my banishment not even see
my kindred nor set foot in my own country,
or otherwise my fate is to be yoked   825
in marriage with my mother and kill my father,
Polybus who begot me and who reared me?
Would not one rightly judge and say that on me
these things were sent by some malignant god?
O no, no, no—O holy majesty   830
of god on high, may I not see that day!
May I be gone out of men's sight before
I see the deadly taint of this disaster
come upon me.

CHORUS LEADER
    My lord, we fear this too. But till this man
    is here and you have heard his story, hope.   835

OEDIPUS

    Yes, I have just this much of hope as well:
    to wait until the herdsman comes.

JOCASTA

                               And what
    will you want with him, once he has appeared?

OEDIPUS

    I'll tell you; if I find that his story is
    the same as yours, I will be clear of guilt.   840

JOCASTA

    What in particular did you learn from my story?

OEDIPUS

    You said that he spoke of highway robbers who
    killed Laius. Now if he still uses that
    same number, I was not the one who killed him.
    One man cannot be the same as many.
    But if he speaks clearly of one man on his own,   845
    indeed the guilty balance tilts toward me.

JOCASTA

    Be sure, at least, that this was how he told the story;
    and he cannot unsay this now, for everyone
    in the city heard it—not just I alone.   850
    But even if he turns from what he said then,
    not ever will he prove, my lord, that rightly
    the murder of Laius squares with Apollo's words,
    Apollo, who declared that by his son
    from me he would be killed. And yet
    that poor creature surely did not kill him—   855
    for he himself died first. As far as prophecy
    goes, henceforward I won't look to the right
    nor to the left hand either.

OEDIPUS

Your opinion's sound. But yet, send someone for   860
the peasant to bring him here; do not neglect it.

JOCASTA

I will send, and quickly. Now let us go indoors.
I will do nothing except what pleases you.

(Exit, into the palace.)

CHORUS [*singing*]

STROPHE A

May destiny ever find me
pious in word and deed
prescribed by the laws that live on high: 865
laws begotten in the clear air of heaven,
whose only father is Olympus;
no mortal nature brought them to birth,
no forgetfulness shall lull them to sleep;   870
for god is great in them and grows not old.

ANTISTROPHE A

Insolence breeds the tyrant, insolence
if it is glutted with a surfeit, unseasonable, unprofitable,
climbs to the rooftop and plunges   875
sheer down to the ruin that must be,
and there its feet are no service.
But I pray that the god may never   880
abolish the eager ambition that profits the state.
For I shall never cease to hold the god as our protector.

STROPHE B

If a man walks with haughtiness
of hand or word and gives no heed   885
to Justice and the shrines of gods
despises—may an evil doom
smite him for his ill-starred pride of heart!—
if he reaps gains without justice
and will not hold from impiety   890

and his fingers itch for untouchable things.
When such things are done, what man shall contrive
to shield his life from the shafts of the god?
When such deeds are held in honor, 895
why should I honor the gods in the dance?

ANTISTROPHE B

No longer to the holy place,
to the navel of earth I'll go
to worship, nor to Abae 900
nor to Olympia,
unless the oracles are proved to fit,
for all men's hands to point at.
O Zeus, if you are rightly called
the sovereign lord, all-mastering,
let this not escape you nor your ever-living power! 905
The oracles concerning Laius
are old and dim and men regard them not.
Apollo is nowhere clear in honor; the gods' service perishes. 910

(Enter Jocasta from the palace, carrying garlands.)

JOCASTA

Lords of the land, I have had the thought to go
to the gods' temples, bringing in my hand
garlands and gifts of incense, as you see.
For Oedipus excites himself too much
with all kinds of worries, not conjecturing, 915
like a man of sense, what will be from what was,
but he is always at the speaker's mercy,
when he speaks terrors. I can do no good
by my advice, and so I come as suppliant
to you, Lycian Apollo, who are nearest. 920
These are the symbols of my prayer and this
my prayer: grant us escape free of the curse.
Now when we look to him we are all afraid;
he's pilot of our ship and he is frightened.

(Enter Messenger, from the side.)

MESSENGER

Might I learn from you, sirs, where is the house of Oedipus?   925
Or better, if you know, where is the king himself?

CHORUS LEADER

This is his house and he is within; the lady
here is his wife and mother of his children.

MESSENGER

God bless you, lady! God bless your household too!
God bless the noble wife of Oedipus!   930

JOCASTA

And god bless you, sir, for your kind greeting!
What do you want of us that you have come here?
What have you to tell us?

MESSENGER

            Good news, lady.
Good for your house and also for your husband.

JOCASTA

What is your news? And who sent you to us?   935

MESSENGER

I come from Corinth; the news I bring will give you
pleasure, for sure. Perhaps some pain as well.

JOCASTA

What is it, then, this news of double meaning?

MESSENGER

The people of the Isthmus will choose Oedipus
to be their king. That is the rumor there.   940

JOCASTA

But isn't their king still aged Polybus?

MESSENGER

No. He is in his grave. Death has got him.

JOCASTA

Is that the truth? Is Oedipus' father dead?

MESSENGER

May I die myself if it be otherwise!

JOCASTA   *(To a servant.)*

Be quick and run to tell the king the news!   945
O oracles of the gods, where are you now?
It was from this man Oedipus fled, long ago,
lest he should be his murderer! And now, by chance,
he is dead, in the course of nature, not killed by him.

(Enter Oedipus from the palace.)

OEDIPUS

Dearest Jocasta, why have you sent for me?   950

JOCASTA

Listen to this man and when you hear, reflect
on what the god's holy oracles have come to.

OEDIPUS

Who is he? What is his message for me?

JOCASTA

He comes from Corinth and tells us that your father   955
Polybus is no more, but dead and gone.

OEDIPUS

What's this you say, stranger? Tell me yourself.

MESSENGER

If this is what you first want clearly told:
be sure, Polybus has gone down to death.

OEDIPUS

Was it by treachery, or from sickness?   960

MESSENGER

A small thing will put old bodies asleep.

OEDIPUS

So he died of sickness, it seems—poor old man!

MESSENGER

Yes, and of age—the long years he had measured.

OEDIPUS

Ah! Ah! O dear Jocasta, why should one
look to the Pythian hearth? Why should one look   965
to the birds screaming overhead? They prophesied
that I should kill my father! But he's dead,
and hidden deep in earth, and I stand here
who never laid a hand on spear against him —
unless perhaps he died of longing for me,
and thus I am his murderer. But they,   970
the oracles, as they stand—he's taken them
away with him, they're dead as he himself is,
and worthless.

JOCASTA

                         That I already told you before now.

OEDIPUS

You did, but I was misled by my fear.

JOCASTA

Then lay no more of them to heart, not one.   975

OEDIPUS

But surely I must fear my mother's bed?

JOCASTA

Why should man fear since chance is all in all
for him, and he can clearly foreknow nothing?
Best to live lightly, as one can, unthinkingly.
As to your mother's marriage bed—do not   980
feel fear about this: before now, many a man
in his dreams has lain with his own mother.
But he to whom such things are nothing bears
his life most easily.

OEDIPUS

    All that you say would be said perfectly
    if she were dead; but since she lives I must   985
    still fear, although you talk so well, Jocasta.

JOCASTA

    Still in your father's death there's light of comfort?

OEDIPUS

    Great light of comfort; but I fear the living.

MESSENGER

    Who is the woman that makes you afraid?

OEDIPUS

    Merope, old man, Polybus' wife.   990

MESSENGER

    What about her frightens the queen and you?

OEDIPUS

    A terrible oracle, stranger, from the gods.

MESSENGER

    Can it be told? Or does the sacred law
    forbid another to have knowledge of it?

OEDIPUS

    O no! Once on a time Loxias said
    that I should lie with my own mother and   995
    take on my hands the blood of my own father.
    And so for these long years I've lived away
    from Corinth; it has been to my good fortune;
    but yet it's sweet to see the face of parents.

MESSENGER

    This was the fear that drove you out of Corinth?   1000

OEDIPUS

    Old man, I did not wish to kill my father.

MESSENGER

Why should I not free you from this fear, sir,
since I have come to you in all goodwill?

OEDIPUS

You would not find me thankless if you did.

MESSENGER

Why, it was just for this I brought the news—   1005
to earn your thanks when you had come safe home.

OEDIPUS

No, I will never come near my parents.

MESSENGER

Son,
it's very plain you don't know what you're doing.

OEDIPUS

What do you mean, old man? For god's sake, tell me.

MESSENGER

If your homecoming is checked by fears like these.   1010

OEDIPUS

Yes, I'm afraid that Phoebus may prove right.

MESSENGER

Pollution from your parents?

OEDIPUS

Yes, old man;
that is my constant terror.

MESSENGER

Do you know
that all your fears are empty?

OEDIPUS

How is that,
if they are father and mother and I their son?   1015

MESSENGER

Because Polybus was no kin to you in blood.

OEDIPUS

What, was not Polybus my father?

MESSENGER

No more than I but just so much.

OEDIPUS

How can
my father be my father as much as one
that's nothing to me?

MESSENGER

Neither he nor I   1020
begot you.

OEDIPUS

Why then did he call me son?

MESSENGER

A gift he took you from these hands of mine.

OEDIPUS

Did he love so much what he took from another's hand?

MESSENGER

His childlessness before persuaded him.

OEDIPUS

Was I a child you bought or found when I   1025
was given to him?

MESSENGER

On Cithaeron's slopes
in the twisting thickets you were found.

OEDIPUS

And why
were you a traveler in those parts?

MESSENGER

                    I was
in charge of mountain flocks.

OEDIPUS

                             You were a shepherd?
A hireling vagrant?

MESSENGER

                    Yes, but at least at that time   1030
the man that saved your life, son.

OEDIPUS

What ailed me when you took me in your arms?

MESSENGER

In that your ankles should be witnesses.

OEDIPUS

Why do you speak of that old pain?

MESSENGER

                          I loosed you;
the tendons of your feet were pierced and fettered—   1035

OEDIPUS

My swaddling clothes brought me a rare disgrace.

MESSENGER

so that from this you're called your present name.

OEDIPUS

Was this my father's doing or my mother's?
For god's sake, tell me.

MESSENGER

                  I don't know, but he
who gave you to me has more knowledge than I.

OEDIPUS

You yourself did not find me then? You took me
from someone else?

MESSENGER

                Yes, from another shepherd.   1040

OEDIPUS

Who was he? Do you know him well enough
to tell?

MESSENGER

                He was called one of Laius' men.

OEDIPUS

You mean the king who reigned here in the old days?

MESSENGER

Yes, he was that man's shepherd.

OEDIPUS

                      Is he alive   1045
still, so that I could see him?

MESSENGER

                    You who live here
would know that best.

OEDIPUS

                  Do any of you here
know of this shepherd whom he speaks about
in town or in the fields? Tell me. It's time
that this was found out once for all.   1050

CHORUS LEADER

I think he is none other than the peasant
whom you have sought to see already; but
Jocasta here can tell us best of that.

OEDIPUS

Jocasta, do you know about this man
whom we have sent for? Is that the man he mentions?   1055

JOCASTA

Why ask of whom he spoke? Don't give it heed;

nor try to keep in mind what has been said.
It will be wasted labor.

OEDIPUS

With such clues
I could not fail to bring my birth to light.

JOCASTA

I beg you—do not hunt this out—I beg you,   1060
if you have any care for your own life.
What I am suffering is enough.

OEDIPUS

Keep up
your heart, Jocasta. Though I'm proved a slave,
thrice slave, and though my mother be thrice slave,
you'll not be shown to be of lowly lineage.

JOCASTA

O be persuaded by me, I entreat you;
do not do this.

OEDIPUS

I will not be persuaded to let be   1065
the chance of finding out the whole thing clearly.

JOCASTA

It is because I wish you well that I
give you this counsel—and it's the best counsel.

OEDIPUS

Then the best counsel vexes me, and has
for some while since.

JOCASTA

O Oedipus, god help you!
God keep you from the knowledge of who you are!

OEDIPUS

Here, someone, go and fetch the shepherd for me;
and let her find her joy in her rich family!   1070

JOCASTA

O Oedipus, unhappy Oedipus!
that is all I can call you, and the last thing
that I shall ever call you.

(Exit Jocasta into the palace.)

CHORUS LEADER

Why has the queen gone, Oedipus, in wild
grief rushing from us? I am afraid that trouble
will break out of this silence.   1075

OEDIPUS

Break out what will! I at least shall be
willing to see my ancestry, though humble.
Perhaps she is ashamed of my low birth,
for she has all a woman's high-flown pride.
But I account myself a child of Fortune,   1080
beneficent goddess, and I shall not be
dishonored. Fortune's the mother from whom I spring;
the months, my brothers, marked me, now as small,
and now again as mighty. Such is my breeding,
and I shall never prove so false to it,
as not to find the secret of my birth.   1085

CHORUS [*singing*]

STROPHE

If I am a prophet and wise of heart
you shall not fail, Cithaeron,
by the limitless sky, you shall not!—
to know that tomorrow's full moon   1090
shall honor you as Oedipus' compatriot,
his mother and nurse at once;
and that you shall be honored in dancing by us,
for rendering service to our king.   1095
Apollo, to whom we cry, find these things pleasing!

ANTISTROPHE

Who was it bore you, child? One of

the long-lived nymphs who lay with Pan—   1100
the father who treads the hills?
Or was your mother a bride of Loxias? The grassy slopes
are all of them dear to him. Or perhaps Cyllene's king
or the Bacchants' god that lives on the tops   1105
of the hills received you, a gift from some
one of the dark-eyed Nymphs, with whom he mostly plays?

(Enter an old Herdsman from the side, led by Oedipus' servants.)

OEDIPUS

If someone like myself who never met him   1110
may make a guess—I think this is the herdsman,
whom we were seeking. His old age is consonant
with the other's. And besides, the men who bring him
I recognize as my own servants. But you
perhaps may better me in knowledge since   1115
you've seen the man before.

CHORUS LEADER
                                    You can be sure
I recognize him. For if Laius
had ever an honest shepherd, this was he.

OEDIPUS

You, sir, from Corinth, I must ask you first,
is this the man you spoke of?

MESSENGER
                                    This is he   1120
before your eyes.

OEDIPUS
                        Old man, look here at me
and tell me what I ask you. Were you ever
a servant of King Laius?

HERDSMAN
                        I was—
no slave he bought but reared in his own house.

OEDIPUS

What did you do as work? How did you live?

HERDSMAN

Most of my life was spent among the flocks.   1125

OEDIPUS

In what part of the country did you live?

HERDSMAN

Cithaeron and the places near to it.

OEDIPUS

And somewhere there perhaps you knew this man?

HERDSMAN

What was he doing? What man?

OEDIPUS

                              This man here,
have you had any dealings with him?   1130

HERDSMAN

                              No—
not such that I can quickly call to mind.

MESSENGER

That is no wonder, master. But I'll help him
remember what he does not know. For I know
that he knows well the country of Cithaeron,
how he with two flocks, I with one, together   1135
kept company for three years—six months each year—
from spring till autumn time. When winter came
I drove my flocks back to our fold, back home,
while this man, he drove his to Laius' steadings.
Am I right or not in what I say we did?   1140

HERDSMAN

You're right—although it's a long time ago.

MESSENGER

Do you remember giving me a baby
to bring up as my foster child?

HERDSMAN

What's this?
Why do you ask this question?

MESSENGER

Look old man,
here he is—here's the man who was that child!   1145

HERDSMAN

Death take you! Won't you hold your tongue?

OEDIPUS

No, no,
do not find fault with him, old man. Your words
are more at fault than his.

HERDSMAN

O best of masters,
how do I give offense?

OEDIPUS

When you refuse
to speak about the child of whom he asks you.   1150

HERDSMAN

He speaks out of his ignorance, without meaning.

OEDIPUS

If you'll not talk to gratify me, you
will talk with pain to urge you.

HERDSMAN

O please, sir,
don't hurt an old man, sir.

OEDIPUS   *(To the servants.)*

Here, one of you,
twist his hands behind him.

HERDSMAN

                          Why, god help me, why?
What do you want to know?   1155

OEDIPUS

                          You gave a child
to him—the child he asked you of?

HERDSMAN

                          I did.
I wish I'd died the day I did.

OEDIPUS

              You will
unless you tell me truly.

HERDSMAN

                          And I'll die
far worse if I should tell you.

OEDIPUS

                          This fellow   1160
is bent on more delays, as it would seem.

HERDSMAN

O no, no! I have told you that I gave it.

OEDIPUS

Where did you get this child from? Was it your own
or did you get it from another?

HERDSMAN

              Not
my own at all; I had it from someone.

OEDIPUS

One of these citizens? And from what house?

HERDSMAN

O master, please—I beg you, master, please   1165
don't ask me more.

OEDIPUS

You're a dead man if I
ask you again.

HERDSMAN

The child came from the house
of Laius.

OEDIPUS

A slave? Or born from himself?

HERDSMAN

O god, I am on the brink of frightful speech.

OEDIPUS

And I of frightful hearing. But I must hear.   1170

HERDSMAN

The child was called his child; but she within,
your wife would tell you best how all this was.

OEDIPUS

She gave it to you?

HERDSMAN

Yes she did, my lord.

OEDIPUS

To do what with it?

HERDSMAN

Make away with it.

OEDIPUS

She was so hard—its mother?   1175

HERDSMAN

Aye, through fear
of evil oracles.

OEDIPUS

Which?

HERDSMAN
            They said that he
    should kill his parents.

OEDIPUS
                How was it that you
    gave it away to this old man?

HERDSMAN
                O master,
    I pitied it, and thought that I could send it
    off to another country: and this man
    was from another country. But he saved it   1180
    for the most terrible troubles. If you are
    the man he says you are, you're bred to misery.

OEDIPUS
    O, O, O, they will all come,
    all come out clearly! Light of the sun, let me
    look upon you no more after today!
    I who first saw the light bred of a coupling
    accursed, and accursed in my living
    with them I lived with, cursed in my killing.   1185

    (Exit Oedipus into the palace. All but the Chorus depart to the side.)

CHORUS [*singing*]
                    STROPHE A
    O generations of men, how I
    count you as equal with those who live
    not at all!
    What man, what man on earth wins more   1190
    of happiness than a seeming
    and after that falling away?
    Oedipus, you are my pattern of this,
    Oedipus, you and your fate!   1195
    Luckless Oedipus, as I look at you,
    I count nothing in human affairs happy.

Inasmuch as you shot your bolt
beyond the others and won the prize
of happiness complete—
O Zeus—and killed and reduced to naught
the hooked taloned maid of the riddling speech,   1200
standing a tower against death for my land;
hence you are called my king and hence
have been honored the highest of all
honors; and hence you ruled
in the great city of Thebes.

STROPHE B

But now whose tale is more miserable?
Who is there lives with a savager fate?°   1205
Whose troubles so reverse his life as his?
O Oedipus, the famous prince
for whom the same great harbor
the same both for father and son
sufficed for bridal bed,   1210
how, O how, have the furrows ploughed
by your father endured to bear you, poor wretch,
and remain silent so long?

ANTISTROPHE B

Time who sees all has found you out
against your will; judges your marriage accursed,
begetter and begotten at one in it.   1215
O child of Laius,
would I had never seen you.
I weep for you and cry
a dirge of lamentation.
To speak directly, I drew my breath   1220
from you at the first and so now I lull
my eyes to sleep with your name.

(Enter a Second Messenger, from the palace.)

SECOND MESSENGER

    O princes always honored by our country,
    what deeds you'll hear of and what horrors see,
    what grief you'll feel, if you as trueborn Thebans   1225
    care for the house of Labdacus's sons.
    No river, not Phasis nor Ister, can purge this house,
    I think, with all their streams, such things
    it hides, such evils shortly will bring forth
    into the light, evils done on purpose;   1230
    and troubles hurt the most
    when they prove self-inflicted.

CHORUS LEADER

    What we had known before did not fall short
    of bitter groaning; now what's more to tell?

SECOND MESSENGER

    Shortest to hear and say—our glorious queen
    Jocasta's dead.   1235

CHORUS LEADER

               Unhappy woman! How?

SECOND MESSENGER

    By her own hand. You're spared the greatest pain
    of what was done—you did not see the sight.
    Yet insofar as I remember it
    you'll hear the sufferings of our unlucky queen.   1240
        When she came raging into the house she went
    straight to her marriage bed, tearing her hair
    with both her hands, and slammed the bedroom doors
    behind her shut, crying upon Laius
    long dead—"Do you remember, Laius,   1245
    that night long past which bred a child for us
    to send you to your death and leave
    a mother making children with her son?"
    And then she groaned and cursed the bed in which
    she brought forth husband by her husband, children   1250

by her own child, an infamous double bond.
    How after that she died I do not know—
for Oedipus distracted us from seeing.
He burst upon us shouting and we looked
to him as he paced frantically around,
begging us always: "Give me a sword, I say,   1255
to find this wife no wife, this mother's womb,
this field of double sowing whence I sprang
and where I sowed my children!" As he raved
some god showed him the way—none of us there.
Bellowing terribly and led by some   1260
invisible guide he rushed on the two doors—
wrenching the bending bolts out of their sockets,
he charged inside. There, there, we saw his wife
hanging, the twisted rope around her neck.
When he saw her, he cried out fearfully   1265
and cut the dangling noose. Then, as she lay,
poor woman, on the ground, what happened after,
was terrible to see. He tore the brooches—
the gold chased brooches fastening her robe—
away from her and lifting them up high
dashed them on his own eyeballs, shrieking out   1270
such things as: "You will never see the crime
I have committed or had done upon me!
Dark eyes, now in the days to come look on
forbidden faces, do not recognize
those whom you long for"—with such imprecations
he struck his eyes again and yet again   1275
with the brooches. And the bleeding eyeballs gushed
and stained his cheeks—no sluggish oozing drops
but a black rain and bloody hail poured down.
    So it has broken—and not on one head alone°   1280
but troubles mixed for husband and for wife.
The fortune of the days gone by was true
good fortune—but today groans and destruction

and death and shame—of all ills that can be named
not one is missing.   1285

CHORUS LEADER
  Is he now in any ease from pain?

SECOND MESSENGER
                    He shouts
  for someone to unbar the doors and show him
  to all the men of Thebes, his father's killer,
  his mother's—no I cannot say the word,
  it is unholy—for he'll cast himself,   1290
  out of the land, he says, and not remain
  to bring a curse upon his house, the curse
  he called upon it in his proclamation. But
  he wants for strength, aye, and someone to guide him;
  his sickness is too great to bear. You, too,
  will be shown that. The bolts are opening.
  Soon you will see a sight to waken pity   1295
  even in one who feels disgust or hatred.

                    (Enter the blinded Oedipus, from the palace.)

CHORUS [chanting]
  This is a terrible sight for men to see!
  I never encountered a worse horror!
  Poor wretch, what madness came upon you?   1300
  What evil spirit leaped upon your life
  to your ill luck—a leap beyond man's strength!
  Indeed I pity you, but I cannot
  look at you, though there's much I want to ask
  and much to learn and much to see.   1305
  I shudder at the sight of you.

OEDIPUS [singing in what follows, while the Chorus speaks]
  O, O,
  where am I going? Where is my voice

borne on the wind to and fro?   1310
Spirit, how far have you sprung?

CHORUS LEADER

To a terrible place which men's ears
may not hear of, nor their eyes see it.

OEDIPUS

STROPHE A

Darkness!
Horror of darkness enfolding, resistless, unspeakable visitant sped   1315
by an ill wind in haste!°
Madness and stabbing pain and memory
of my evils!

CHORUS LEADER

In such misfortunes it's no wonder
if double weighs the burden of your grief.   1320

OEDIPUS

ANTISTROPHE A

My friend,
you are the only one steadfast, the only one that attends on me;
you still stay nursing the blind man.
Your care is not unnoticed. I recognize   1325
your voice, although this darkness is my world.

CHORUS LEADER

Doer of dreadful deeds, how did you dare
so far to do despite to your own eyes?
What spirit urged you to it?

OEDIPUS

STROPHE B

It was Apollo, friends, Apollo,
that brought this bitter bitterness, my sorrows to completion.   1330
But the hand that struck me
was none but my own.
Why should I see
whose vision showed me nothing sweet to see?   1335

CHORUS [now singing]
  These things are as you say.

OEDIPUS

  What can I see to love?
  What greeting can touch my ears with joy?
  Take me away, and haste—to a place out of the way!   1340
  Take me away, my friends, the greatly miserable,
  the most accursed, whom the gods too hate   1345
  above all men on earth!

CHORUS LEADER
  Unhappy in your mind and your misfortune,
  would I had never known you!

OEDIPUS

                    ANTISTROPHE B
  Curse on the man° who took
  the cruel bonds from off my legs, as I lay there.   1350
  He stole me from death and saved me,
  no kindly service.
  Had I died then,
  I would not be so burdensome to friends or to myself.   1355

CHORUS
  I, too, could have wished it had been so.

OEDIPUS

  Then I would not have come
  to kill my father and marry my mother infamously.
  Now I am godless and child of impurity,   1360
  begetter in the same seed that created my wretched self.
  If there is any ill worse than ill,   1365
  that is the lot of Oedipus.

CHORUS LEADER
  I cannot say your remedy was good;
  you would be better dead than blind and living.

OEDIPUS [*now speaking*]

  What I have done here was best done—don't tell me
  otherwise, do not give me further counsel.   1370
  I do not know with what eyes I could look
  upon my father when I die and go
  under the earth, nor yet my wretched mother—
  those two to whom I have done things deserving
  worse punishment than hanging. Would the sight
  of children, bred as mine are, gladden me?   1375
  No, not these eyes, never. And my city,
  its towers and sacred places of the gods,
  where I was raised as the noblest man in Thebes,   1380
  of these I robbed my miserable self
  when I commanded all to drive him out,
  the criminal since proved by the gods impure
  and of the race of Laius.
  To this guilt I bore witness against myself—
  with what eyes was I to look upon my people?   1385
  No. If there were a means to choke the fountain
  of hearing I would not have stayed my hand
  from locking up my miserable carcass,
  seeing and hearing nothing; it is sweet
  to keep our thoughts out of the range of hurt.   1390
      Cithaeron, why did you receive me? Why
  having received me did you not kill me straight?
  And so I'd not have shown to men my birth.
  O Polybus and Corinth and the house,
  the old house that I used to call my father's—   1395
  what fairness you were nurse to, and what foulness
  festered beneath! Now I am found to be
  evil and a son of evil. Crossroads,
  and hidden glade, oak and the narrow way
  at the crossroads that drank my father's blood—   1400
  my own blood—from my hands, do you remember
  still what I did as you looked on, and what
  I did when I came here? O marriage, marriage!

you bred me and again when you had bred
you produced the same seed again and displayed to men   1405
fathers, brothers, children, an incestuous brood,
brides, wives, and mothers, all the foulest deeds
that can be in this world of ours.

Come—it's unfit to say what is unfit
to do.—I beg of you in the gods' name hide me   1410
somewhere outside your country, yes, or kill me,
or throw me into the sea, to be forever
out of your sight. Approach and deign to touch me
for all my wretchedness, and do not fear.
No man but I can bear my evil doom.   1415

(Enter Creon, from the side, with attendants.)

CHORUS LEADER
Here Creon comes in fit time to perform
or give advice in what you ask of us.
Creon is left sole ruler in your stead.

OEDIPUS
Creon! Creon! What shall I say to him?
How can I justly hope that he will trust me?   1420
In what is past I have been proved toward him
an utter liar.

CREON
                                    Oedipus, I've come
not so that I might laugh at you nor taunt you
with evil of the past.

(To attendants.)

                                    But even if you men
have no more shame before the face of men,
reverence at least the flame that gives all life,   1425
our lord the Sun, and do not show unveiled
to him pollution such that neither land
nor holy rain nor light of day can welcome.

Be quick and take him in. It is most decent
that only kin should see and hear the troubles   1430
of kin.

OEDIPUS

                         I beg you, since you've torn me from
my dreadful expectations and have come
in a most noble spirit to a man
that has used you vilely—do a thing for me.
I shall speak for your own good, not for my own.

CREON

What do you need that you would ask of me?   1435

OEDIPUS

Drive me from here with all the speed you can
to where I may not hear a human voice.

CREON

Be sure, I would have done this had not I
wished first of all to learn from the god the course
of action I should follow.

OEDIPUS

                            But his word   1440
has been quite clear to let the parricide,
the sinner, die.

CREON

                      Yes, that indeed was said.
But in the present need we had best discover
what we should do.

OEDIPUS

                     And will you ask about
a man so wretched?

CREON

                     Now even you will trust   1445
the god.

OEDIPUS

          So. I command you—and will beseech you—
to her that lies inside that house give burial
as you would have it; she is yours and rightly
you will perform the rites for her. For me—
never let this my father's city have me   1450
living a dweller in it. Leave me live
in the mountains where Cithaeron is that's called
my mountain, which my mother and my father
while they were living would have made my tomb.
So I may die by their decree who sought
indeed to kill me. Yet I know this much: 1455
no sickness and no other thing will kill me.
I would not have been saved from death if not
for some strange evil fate. Well, let my fate
go where it will.

                    Creon, you need not care
about my sons; they're men and so wherever   1460
they are, they will not lack a livelihood.
But my two girls—so sad and pitiful—
whose table never stood apart from mine,
and everything I touched they always shared—   1465
O Creon, have a thought for them! And most
I wish that you might allow me to touch them
and sorrow with them.

        (Enter Antigone and Ismene from the palace.)

O my lord! O true noble Creon! May I
really touch them, as when I saw?   1470
What shall I say?
Can I hear them sobbing—my two darlings!—
and Creon has had pity and has sent me
what I loved most?
Am I right?   1475

CREON

You're right: it was I gave you this

because I knew from old days how you loved them
as I see now.

OEDIPUS

God bless you for it, Creon,
and may god guard you better on your road
than he did me!
                              O children,
where are you? Come here, come to my hands,   1480
a brother's hands which turned your father's eyes,
those bright eyes you knew once, to what you see,
a father seeing nothing, knowing nothing,
begetting you from his own source of life.   1485
I weep for you—I cannot see your faces—
I weep when I think of the bitterness
there will be in your lives, how you must live
before the world. At what assemblages
of citizens will you attend? To what
festivals will you go and not come home   1490
in tears instead of sharing in the holiday?
And when you're ripe for marriage, who will he be,
the man who'll risk to take such infamy
as shall cling to my children, to bring hurt
on them and those that marry with them? What   1495
evil is not there? "Your father killed his father
and sowed the seed where he had sprung himself
and begot you out of the womb that held him."
Such insults you will hear. Then who will marry you?   1500
No one, my children; clearly you are doomed
to waste away in barrenness unmarried.
        Son of Menoeceus, since you are all the father
left these two girls, and we, their parents, both
are dead to them—do not allow them to wander   1505
like beggars, poor and husbandless.
They are of your own blood.
And do not make them equal with myself

in wretchedness; for you can see them now
so young, so utterly alone, save for you only.
Touch my hand, noble Creon, and say yes.   1510
        If you were older, children, and were wiser,
there's much advice I'd give you. But as it is,
let this be what you pray: to find a life
wherever there is opportunity
to live, a better life than was your father's.

CREON

Your tears have had enough of scope; now go within the
    house.   1515

OEDIPUS

I must obey, though bitter of heart.

CREON

                In season, all is good.

OEDIPUS

Do you know on what conditions I obey?

CREON

                                You tell me them,
and I shall know them when I hear.

OEDIPUS

                That you shall send me out
to live away from Thebes.

CREON

                That gift you must ask of the god.

OEDIPUS

But I'm now hated by the gods.

CREON

                So quickly you'll obtain your prayer.

OEDIPUS

You consent then?   1520

CREON

        What I do not mean, I do not use to say.

OEDIPUS

Now lead me away from here.

CREON

        Let go the children, then, and come.

OEDIPUS

Do not take them from me.

CREON

        Do not seek to be master in everything,
for the things you mastered did not follow you throughout
   your life.

(Creon and Oedipus depart.)

CHORUS°

You that live in my ancestral Thebes, behold this Oedipus—
him who knew the famous riddles and was a man most
   masterful;   1525
not a citizen who did not look with envy on his lot—
see him now and see the breakers of misfortune swallow him!
Look upon that last day always. Count no mortal happy till
he has passed the final limit of his life secure from pain.   1530

ANTIGONE

SOPHOCLES
Translated by Elizabeth Wyckoff

INTRODUCTION TO SOPHOCLES' ANTIGONE

Antigone was probably produced in 442 BCE. Though the part of the saga of Thebes with which it deals is subsequent to the action of *Oedipus the King* and also *Oedipus at Colonus*, the drama itself was certainly the earliest written of the three, which therefore do not compose a formal trilogy.

The audience which first saw the play was already familiar with the main outlines of the story of Oedipus' sons, Eteocles and Polynices: how they quarreled over their inheritance and the kingship in Thebes; how Polynices, aided by six Argive champions, led an assault on his home city (the Seven against Thebes); how that assault was defeated, with the two brothers killing each other; and how the new ruler in Thebes, Creon (brother of Oedipus' mother / wife, Jocasta), forbade burial to some or all of the attackers. (In Sophocles' play, it is just Polynices' corpse that is denied burial.) But the details of Sophocles' plot seem to have been largely new, and unexpected. Antigone herself may be his own invention as a character in the story, and the central theme of her defiance of Creon's edict seems to be unprecedented as well; likewise the crucial detail of her betrothal to Creon's son, Haemon. The contrast with *Oedipus the King*, a play in which all is known and almost none of the events are unexpected to the audience, is striking. Yet *Antigone* contains its share of tragic irony too, through the shape of the developing action, as Creon, acting always in the belief that he is promoting the good of the whole community, ends up—too late—completely reversing his own policy and yet still destroying all those who are most dear to him.

ANTIGONE

Characters   ANTIGONE, daughter of Oedipus
    ISMENE, her sister
    CHORUS of Theban elders
    CREON, king of Thebes
    A GUARD
    HAEMON, son of Creon
    TEIRESIAS
    A MESSENGER
    EURYDICE, wife of Creon

Scene: Thebes, before the royal palace.

                    (Antigone and Ismene enter from the palace.)

ANTIGONE
    My sister, my Ismene, do you know
    of any suffering from our father sprung
    that Zeus does not achieve for us survivors?
    There's nothing grievous, nothing full of doom,°
    or shameful, or dishonored, I've not seen: 5
    your sufferings and mine.
    And now, what of this edict which they say
    the commander has proclaimed to the whole people?
    Have you heard anything? Or don't you know
    that our enemies' trouble comes upon our friends?   10

ISMENE
    I've heard no word, Antigone, of our friends,

not sweet nor bitter, since that single moment
when we two lost two brothers
who died on one day by a double blow.
And since the Argive army went away   15
this very night, I have no further news
of fortune or disaster for myself.

ANTIGONE

I knew it well, and brought you from the house
for just this reason, that you alone may hear.

ISMENE

What is it? Clearly some news has clouded you.   20

ANTIGONE

It has indeed. Creon will give the one
of our two brothers honor in the tomb;
the other none. Eteocles, with just observance treated,
as law provides he has hidden under earth   25
to have full honor with the dead below.
But Polyneices' corpse who died in pain,
they say he has proclaimed to the whole town
that none may bury him and none bewail,
but leave him, unwept, untombed, a rich sweet sight
for the hungry birds' beholding and devouring.   30
        Such orders they say the worthy Creon gives
to you and me—yes, yes, I say to *me*—
and that he's coming to proclaim it clear
to those who know it not.
Further: he has the matter so at heart   35
that anyone who dares attempt the act
will die by public stoning in the town.
So there you have it and you soon will show
if you are noble, or worthless, despite your high birth.

ISMENE

If things have reached this stage, what can I do,
poor sister, that will help to make or mend?   40

ANTIGONE

Think, will you share my labor and my act?

ISMENE

What will you risk? And where is your intent?

ANTIGONE

Will you take up that corpse along with me?

ISMENE

To bury him you mean, when it's forbidden?

ANTIGONE

My brother, and yours, though you may wish he were not.°   45
I never shall be found to be his traitor.

ISMENE

O reckless one, when Creon spoke against it!

ANTIGONE

It's not for him to keep me from my own.

ISMENE

Alas. Remember, sister, how our father
perished abhorred, ill-famed: 50
himself with his own hand, through his own curse
destroyed both eyes.
Remember next his mother and his wife
finishing life in the shame of the twisted noose.
And third, two brothers on a single day,   55
poor creatures, murdering, a common doom
each with his arm accomplished on the other.
And now look at the two of us alone.
We'll perish terribly if we violate law
and try to cross the royal vote and power.   60
We must remember that we two are women,
so not to fight with men;
and that since we are subject to stronger power
we must hear these orders, or any that may be worse.

So I shall ask of them beneath the earth   65
forgiveness, for in these things I am forced,
and shall obey the men in power. I know
that wild and futile action makes no sense.

ANTIGONE

I wouldn't urge it. And if now you wished
to act, you wouldn't please me as a partner.   70
Be what you want to; but that man shall I
bury. For me, the doer, death is best.
Loving, I shall lie with him, yes, with my loved one,
when I have dared the crime of piety.
Longer the time in which to please the dead
than the time with those up here.   75
There shall I lie forever. You may see fit
to keep from honor what the gods have honored.

ISMENE

I shall do no dishonor. But to act
against the citizens, that's beyond my means.

ANTIGONE

That's your excuse. Now I go, to heap   80
the burial mound for him, my dearest brother.

ISMENE

Oh my poor sister. How I fear for you!

ANTIGONE

For me, don't worry. You clear your own fate.

ISMENE

At least give no one notice of this act;
you keep it hidden, and I'll do the same.   85

ANTIGONE

Dear gods! Denounce me. I shall hate you more
if silent, not proclaiming this to all.

ISMENE

You have a hot mind over chilly things.

ANTIGONE

I know I please those whom I most should please.

ISMENE

If but you can. You crave what can't be done.   90

ANTIGONE

And so, when strength runs out, I shall give over.

ISMENE

Wrong from the start, to chase what cannot be.

ANTIGONE

If that's your saying, I shall hate you first,
and next the dead will hate you in all justice.
But let me and my own ill counseling   95
suffer this terror. I shall suffer nothing
so great as to stop me dying with honor.

ISMENE

Go, since you want to. But know this: you go
senseless indeed, but loved by those who love you.

> (*Exit Ismene into the palace. Exit Antigone to one
> side. Enter the Chorus from the other side.*)

CHORUS [*singing*]

STROPHE A

*Sun's own radiance, fairest light ever shone on the seven gates of
    Thebes,*   100
then did you shine, O golden day's
eye, coming over Dirce's stream,   105
on the man who had come from Argos with all his armor
running now in headlong fear as you shook his bridle free.

[*chanting*]
He was stirred by the dubious quarrel of Polyneices.   110

So, screaming shrill,
like an eagle over the land he flew,
covered with white-snow wing,
with many weapons,   115
with horse-hair crested helms.

ANTISTROPHE A [*singing*]
He who had stood above our halls, gaping about our seven gates,
with that circle of blood-thirsting spears:
gone, without our blood in his jaws,   120
before the torch took hold on our tower crown.
Rattle of war at his back; hard the fight for the dragon's foe.   125

[*chanting*]
The boasts of a proud tongue are for Zeus to hate.
So seeing them streaming on
in insolent clangor of gold,   130
he struck with hurling fire him who rushed
for the high wall's top,
hoping to yell out "victory."

STROPHE B [*singing*]
Swinging, striking the earth he fell
fire in hand, who in mad attack,   135
had raged against us with blasts of hate.
He failed. And differently from one to another
on both sides great Ares dealt his blows about,
first in our war team.   140

[*chanting*]
The captains assigned for seven gates
fought with our seven and left behind
their brazen arms as an offering
to Zeus who is turner of battle.
All but those two wretches, sons of one man,
one mother's sons, who planted their spears   145
each against each and found the share
of a common death together.

Great-named Victory comes to us
answering Thebe's warrior joy.
Let us forget the wars just done   150
and visit the shrines of the gods,
all, with night-long dance which Bacchus will lead,
he who shakes Thebe's acres.

                              (*Creon enters from the side.*)

[*chanting*]

    Now here he comes, the king of the land,   155
    Creon, Menoeceus' son,
    newly appointed by the gods' new fate.
    What plan that beats about his mind
    has made him call this council session,   160
    sending his summons to all?

CREON

My friends, the very gods who shook the state
with mighty surge have set it straight again.
So now I sent for you, chosen from all,
first, because I knew you constant in respect   165
to Laius' royal power; and again
when Oedipus had set the state to rights,
and when he perished, you were faithful still
in mind to the descendants of the dead.
When they two perished by a double fate,   170
on one day struck and striking and defiled
each by each other's hand, now it comes that I
hold all the power and the royal throne
through close connection with the perished men.
    You cannot learn of any man the soul,   175
the mind, and the intent until he shows
his practice of the government and law.
For I believe that he who controls the state
if he holds not to the best plans of all,

but locks his tongue up through some kind of fear,   180
he is worst of all who are or were.
And he who counts another greater friend
than his own fatherland, I put him nowhere.
So I—may Zeus all-seeing always know it—
could not keep silent as disaster crept   185
upon the town, destroying hope of safety.
Nor could I count the enemy of the land
friend to myself, not I who know so well
that it's she, the land, who saves us, sailing straight,
and only so can we have friends at all.   190
      With such good rules shall I enlarge our state.
And now I have proclaimed their brother-edict.
In the matter of the sons of Oedipus,
citizens, know: Eteocles who died,
defending this our town with champion spear,   195
is to be covered in the grave and granted
all holy rites we give the noble dead.
But his brother Polyneices, whom I name
the exile who came back and sought to burn
his fatherland, the gods of his own kin,   200
who tried to gorge on blood he shared, and lead
the rest of us as slaves—
it is announced that no one in this town
may give him burial or mourn for him.
Leave him unburied, leave his corpse disgraced,   205
a dinner for the birds and for the dogs.
Such is my mind. Never shall I, myself,
honor the wicked and reject the just.
The man who is well-minded to the state
from me in death and life shall have his honor.   210

CHORUS LEADER
This resolution, Creon, is your own,
in the matter of the traitor and the true.

For you can make such rulings as you will
about the living and about the dead.

CREON

Now you be sentinels of the decree.   215

CHORUS LEADER

Order some younger man to take this on.

CREON

Already there are watchers of the corpse.

CHORUS LEADER

What other order would you give us, then?

CREON

Not to take sides with any who disobey.

CHORUS LEADER

No fool is fool to the point of loving death.   220

CREON

Death is the price. But often we have known
men to be ruined by the hope of profit.

(Enter, from the side, a Guard.)

GUARD

My lord, I cannot claim I'm out of breath
from rushing here with light and hasty step,
for I had many haltings in my thought   225
making me double back upon my road.
My mind kept saying many things to me:
"Why go where you will surely pay the price?"
"Fool, are you halting? And if Creon learns
from someone else, how shall you not be hurt?"   230
Turning this over, on I dillydallied.
And so a short trip turned itself to long.
Finally, though, my coming here won out.

If what I say is nothing, still I'll say it.
For I come clutching to one single hope   235
that I can't suffer what is not my fate.

CREON

What is it that brings on this gloom of yours?

GUARD

I want to tell you first about myself.
I didn't do it, didn't see who did it.
It isn't right for me to get in trouble.   240

CREON

Your aim is good. You fence the facts around.
It's clear you have some shocking news to tell.

GUARD

Terrible tidings make for long delays.

CREON

Speak out the story, and then get away.

GUARD

I'll tell you. Someone left the corpse just now,   245
burial all accomplished, thirsty dust
strewn on the flesh, the ritual complete.

CREON

What are you saying? What man has dared to do it?

GUARD

I wouldn't know. There were no marks of picks,
no grubbed-out earth. The ground was dry and hard,   250
no trace of wheels. The doer left no sign.
When the first fellow on the day-shift showed us,
we all were sick with wonder.
For he was hidden, not inside a tomb,   255
but light dust upon him, enough to avert pollution;
no wild beast's track, nor track of any hound
having been near, nor was the body torn.

We roared bad words about, guard against guard,   260
almost came to blows. No one was there to stop us.
Each man had done it, nobody had done it
so as to prove it on him—we couldn't tell.
We were prepared to hold to red-hot iron,
to walk through fire, to swear before the gods   265
we hadn't done it, hadn't shared the plan,
when it was plotted or when it was done.
And last, when all our sleuthing came out nowhere,
one fellow spoke, who made our heads to droop
low toward the ground. We couldn't disagree.   270
We couldn't see a chance of getting off.
He said we had to tell you all about it.
We couldn't hide the fact.
So he won out. The lot chose poor old me
to win the prize. So here I am unwilling,   275
quite sure you people hardly want to see me.
Nobody likes the bringer of bad news.

CHORUS LEADER
Lord, while he spoke, my mind kept on debating.
Isn't this action possibly a god's?

CREON
Stop now, before you fill me up with rage,   280
or you'll prove yourself insane as well as old.
Unbearable, your saying that the gods
take any kindly forethought for this corpse.
Would it be they had hidden him away,
honoring his good service, he who came   285
to burn their pillared temples and their wealth,
raze their land, and break apart their laws?
Or have you seen them honor wicked men?
It isn't so.
No, from the first there were some men in town   290
who took the edict hard, and growled against me,
who secretly were shaking their heads, not pulling

honestly in the yoke, no way my friends.
These are the people—oh it's clear to me—
who have bribed these men and brought about the deed.   295
No current standard among men's as bad
as silver currency. This destroys the state;
this drives men from their homes; this wicked teacher
drives solid citizens to acts of shame.
It shows men how to act as criminals   300
and know the deeds of utter unholiness.
But every hired hand who helped in this
has brought on himself the sentence he shall have.

  And further, as I still revere great Zeus,
understand this, I tell you under oath: 305
if you don't find the very man whose hands
buried the corpse and bring him for me to see,
not death alone shall be enough for you
till living, strung up, you make clear the crime.
For the future you'll have learned that profiteering   310
has its rules, and that it doesn't pay
to squeeze a profit out of every source.
For you'll have seen that more men come to doom
through dirty profits than are sustained by them.

GUARD
  May I say something? Or just turn and go?   315

CREON
  Aren't you aware your speech is most unwelcome?

GUARD
  Does it annoy your ears, or your mind?

CREON
  Why are you out to allocate my pain?

GUARD
  The doer hurts your mind. I hurt your ears.

CREON

    You are a quibbling rascal through and through.   320

GUARD

    But anyhow I never did the deed.

CREON

    And you the man who sold your life for money!

GUARD

    Oh!
    How terrible to guess, and guess at lies!

CREON

    Go polish up your guesswork. If you don't
    show me the doers you will have to say   325
    that wicked payments work their own revenge.

GUARD

    Indeed, I pray he's found, but yes or no,
    taken or not as luck may settle it,
    you won't see me returning to this place.
    Saved when I neither hoped nor thought to be,   330
    I owe the gods a mighty debt of thanks.

(Exit Creon into the palace. Exit the Guard by the way he came.)

CHORUS [*singing*]

STROPHE A

Many the wonders but nothing is stranger than man.
This thing crosses the sea in the winter's storm,   335
making his path through the roaring waves.
And she, the greatest of gods, the Earth—
ageless she is, and unwearied—he wears her away
as the ploughs go up and down from year to year   340
and his mules turn up the soil.

ANTISTROPHE A

Lighthearted nations of birds he snares and leads,

wild beast tribes and the salty brood of the sea,   345
with the twisted mesh of his nets, this clever man.
He controls with craft the beasts of the open air,
walkers on hills. The horse with his shaggy mane   350
he holds and harnesses, yoked about the neck,
and the strong bull of the mountain.

STROPHE B

Language, and thought like the wind
and the feelings that govern a city,   355
he has taught himself, and shelter against the cold,
refuge from rain. He can always help himself.
He faces no future helpless. There's only death
that he cannot find an escape from. He has contrived   360
refuge from illnesses once beyond all cure.

ANTISTROPHE B

Clever beyond all dreams
the inventive craft that he has   365
which may drive him one time to good or another to evil.
When he honors the laws of the land and the gods' sworn right
high indeed is his city; but cityless the man   370
who dares to dwell with dishonor. Not by my fireside,
never to share my thoughts, who does these things.   375

(Enter the Guard with Antigone, from the side.)

[Chorus now chanting]
My mind is split at this awful sight.
I know her. I cannot deny
Antigone is here.
Alas, the unhappy girl,
unhappy Oedipus' child.   380
Oh what is the meaning of this?
It cannot be you that they bring
for breaking the royal law,
caught in sheer madness.

GUARD

This is the woman who has done the deed.
We caught her at the burying. Where's the king?   385

(Enter Creon from the palace.)

CHORUS LEADER

Back from the house again just when he's needed.

CREON

What must I measure up to? What has happened?

GUARD

Lord, one should never swear off anything.
Afterthought makes the first resolve a liar.
I could have vowed I wouldn't come back here   390
after your threats, after the storm I faced.
But joy that comes beyond the wildest hope
is bigger than all other pleasure known.
I'm here, though I swore not to be, and bring   395
this girl. We caught her burying the dead.
This time we didn't need to shake the lots;
mine was the luck, all mine.
So now, lord, take her, you, and question her
and prove her as you will. But I am free.
And I deserve full clearance on this charge.   400

CREON

Explain the circumstance of the arrest.

GUARD

She was burying the man. You have it all.

CREON

Is this the truth? And do you grasp its meaning?

GUARD

I saw her burying the very corpse
you had forbidden. Is this adequate?   405

CREON

How was she caught and taken in the act?

GUARD

It was like this: when we got back again
struck with those dreadful threatenings of yours,
we swept away the dust that hid the corpse.   410
We stripped it back to slimy nakedness.
And then we sat to windward on the hill
so as to dodge the smell.
We poked each other up with growling threats
if anyone was careless of his work.
For some time this went on, till it was noon.   415
The sun was high and hot. Then from the earth
up rose a dusty whirlwind to the sky,
filling the plain, smearing the forest leaves,
clogging the upper air. We shut our eyes,   420
sat and endured the plague the gods had sent.
Then the storm left us after a long time.
We saw the girl. She cried the sharp and shrill
cry of a bitter bird which sees the nest
bare where the young birds lay.   425
So this same girl, seeing the body stripped,
cried with great groanings, called out dreadful curses
upon the people who had done the deed.
Soon in her hands she brought the thirsty dust,
and holding high a pitcher of wrought bronze   430
she poured the three libations for the dead.
We saw this and rushed down. We trapped her fast;
and she was calm. We taxed her with the deeds
both past and present. Nothing was denied.   435
And I was glad, and yet I took it hard.
One's own escape from trouble makes one glad;
but bringing friends to trouble is hard grief.
Still, I care less for all these second thoughts
than for the fact that I myself am safe.   440

CREON

You there, whose head is drooping to the ground,
do you admit this, or deny you did it?

ANTIGONE

I say I did it and I don't deny it.

CREON   (To the Guard.)

Take yourself off wherever you wish to go
free of a heavy charge.   445

                                                 (To Antigone.)

You—tell me not at length but in a word.
You knew the order not to do this thing?

ANTIGONE

I knew—of course I knew. The word was plain.

CREON

And still you dared to overstep these laws?

ANTIGONE

For me it was not Zeus who made that order.   450
Nor did that Justice who lives with the gods below
mark out such laws to hold among mankind.
Nor did I think your orders were so strong
that you, a mortal man, could overrun
the gods' unwritten and unfailing laws.   455
Not now, nor yesterday's, they always live,
and no one knows their origin in time.
So not through fear of any man's proud spirit
would I be likely to neglect these laws,
and draw on myself the gods' sure punishment.
    I knew that I must die—how could I not?—   460
even without your edict. If I die
before my time, I say it is a gain.
Who lives in sorrows many as are mine
how shall he not be glad to gain his death?

And so, for me to meet this fate's no grief.   465
But if I left that corpse, my mother's son,
dead and unburied I'd have cause to grieve
as now I grieve not.
And if you think my acts are foolishness
the foolishness may be in a fool's eye.   470

CHORUS LEADER
The girl is fierce. She's her father's child.
She cannot yield to trouble; nor could he.

CREON
These rigid spirits are the first to fall.
The strongest iron, hardened in the fire,   475
most often ends in scraps and shatterings.
Small curbs bring raging horses back to terms:
enslaved to his neighbor, who can think of pride?
This girl was expert in her insolence   480
when she broke bounds beyond established law.
Once she had done it, insolence the second,
to boast her doing, and to laugh in it.
I am no man and she the man instead
if she can have this conquest without pain.   485
She is my sister's child, but were she child
of closer kin than any at my hearth,
she and her sister should not so escape
a dreadful death. I charge Ismene too.
She shared the planning of this burial.   490
Call her outside. I saw her in the house,
maddened, no longer mistress of herself.
The sly intent betrays itself sometimes
before the secret plotters work their wrong.
I hate it too when someone caught in crime   495
then wants to make it seem a lovely thing.

ANTIGONE
Do you want more than my arrest and death?

CREON

No more than that. For that is all I need.

ANTIGONE

Why are you waiting? Nothing that you say
fits with my thought. I pray it never will.   500
Nor will you ever like to hear my words.
And yet what greater glory could I find
than giving my own brother funeral?
All these would say that they approved my act
did fear not mute them.   505
A king is fortunate in many ways,
and most, that he can act and speak at will.

CREON

None of these others see the case this way.

ANTIGONE

They see, and do not say. You have them cowed.

CREON

And you are not ashamed to think alone?   510

ANTIGONE

It is no shame to serve blood relatives.

CREON

Was not he who died on the other side your brother?

ANTIGONE

Full brother, on both sides, my parents' child.

CREON

Your act of grace, in his regard, is crime.

ANTIGONE

The corpse below would never say it was.   515

CREON

When you honor him and the criminal just alike?

ANTIGONE

It was a brother, not a slave, who died.

CREON

Died to destroy this land the other guarded.

ANTIGONE

Death yearns for equal law for all the dead.

CREON

Not that the good and bad draw equal shares.   520

ANTIGONE

Who knows but this is holiness below?

CREON

Never is the enemy, even in death, a friend.

ANTIGONE

I cannot share in hatred, but in love.

CREON

Then go down there, if you must love, and love
the dead. No woman rules me while I live.   525

(Ismene is brought from the palace under guard.)

CHORUS [*chanting*]

> *Look there! Ismene is coming out.*
> *She loves her sister and mourns,*
> *with clouded brow and bloodied cheeks,*
> *tears on her lovely face.*   530

CREON

You, lurking like a viper in the house,
who sucked me dry, while I raised unawares
a twin destruction planned against the throne.
Now tell me, do you say you shared this deed?
Or will you swear you didn't even know?   535

ISMENE

I did the deed if she agrees I did.
I am accessory and share the blame.

ANTIGONE

Justice will not allow this. You did not
wish for a part, nor did I give you one.

ISMENE

You are in trouble, and I'm not ashamed   540
to sail beside you into suffering.

ANTIGONE

Death and the dead, they know whose act it was.
I cannot love a friend whose love's mere words.

ISMENE

Sister, I pray, don't fence me out from honor,
from death with you, and honor done the dead.   545

ANTIGONE

Don't die along with me, nor make your own
that which you did not do. My death's enough.

ISMENE

When you are gone what life can I desire?

ANTIGONE

Love Creon. He's your kinsman and your care.

ISMENE

Why hurt me, when it does yourself no good?   550

ANTIGONE

I also suffer, when I laugh at you.

ISMENE

What further service can I do you now?

ANTIGONE

To save yourself. I shall not envy you.

ISMENE

Alas for me. Am I outside your fate?

ANTIGONE

Yes. For you chose to live when I chose death.   555

ISMENE

At least I was not silent. You were warned.

ANTIGONE

Some will have thought you wiser. Some will not.

ISMENE

And yet the blame is equal for us both.

ANTIGONE

Take heart. You live. My life died long ago.
And that has made me fit to help the dead.   560

CREON

One of these girls has shown her lack of sense
just now. The other had it from her birth.

ISMENE

Yes, king. When people fall in deep distress
their native sense departs, and will not stay.

CREON

You chose your mind's distraction when you chose   565
to work out wickedness with this wicked girl.

ISMENE

What life is there for me to live without her?

CREON

Don't speak of her. For she is here no more.

ISMENE

But will you kill your own son's promised bride?

CREON

Oh, there are other furrows for his plough.

ISMENE

But where the closeness that has bound these two? 570

CREON

Not for my sons will I choose wicked wives.

ISMENE°

Dear Haemon, your father robs you of your rights.

CREON

You and your marriage trouble me too much.

ISMENE

You will take away his bride from your own son?

CREON

Yes. Death will help me break this marriage off. 575

CHORUS LEADER

It seems determined that the girl must die.

CREON

You helped determine it. Now, no delay!
Slaves, take them in. They must be women now.
No more free running.
Even the bold will flee when they see Death 580
drawing in close enough to end their life.

(Antigone and Ismene are taken inside.)

CHORUS [singing]

STROPHE A

Fortunate they whose lives have no taste of pain.
For those whose house is shaken by the gods 585
escape no kind of doom. It extends to all the kin
like the wave that comes when the winds of Thrace
run over the dark of the sea.
The black sand of the bottom is brought from the depth; 590
the beaten cliffs sound back with a hollow cry.

Ancient the sorrow of Labdacus' house, I know.
Dead men's grief comes back, and falls on grief.   595
No generation can free the next.
One of the gods will strike. There is no escape.
So now the light goes out
for the house of Oedipus, while the bloody knife   600
cuts the remaining root,° in folly and the mind's fury.

STROPHE B

What transgression of man, O Zeus, can bind your power?
Not sleep can destroy it who governs all,°   606
nor the weariless months the gods have set. Unaged in time
monarch you rule in Olympus' gleaming light.   610
Near time, far future, and the past,
one law controls them all:
any greatness in human life brings doom.

ANTISTROPHE B

Wandering hope brings help to many men.
But others she tricks with giddy loves,   616
and her quarry knows nothing until he has walked into flame.
Word of wisdom it was when someone said,   620
"The bad looks like the good
to him a god would doom."
Only briefly is that one free from doom.   625

(Haemon enters from the side.)

[chanting]
          Here is Haemon, your one surviving son.
          Does he come in grief at the fate of his bride,
          in pain that he's tricked of his wedding?   630

CREON
     Soon we shall know more than a seer could tell us.
     Son, have you heard the vote condemned your bride?
     And are you here, maddened against your father,
     or are we friends, whatever I may do?

HAEMON

    My father, I am yours. You keep me straight   635
    with your good judgment, which I shall ever follow.
    Nor shall a marriage count for more with me
    than your kind leading.

CREON

    There's my good boy. So should you hold at heart
    and stand behind your father all the way.   640
    It is for this men pray they may beget
    households of dutiful obedient sons,
    who share alike in punishing enemies,
    and give due honor to their father's friends.
    Whoever breeds a child that will not help,   645
    what has he sown but trouble for himself,
    and for his enemies laughter full and free?
    Son, do not let your lust mislead your mind,
    all for a woman's sake, for well you know
    how cold the thing he takes into his arms   650
    who has a wicked woman for his wife.
    What deeper wound than a loved one who is evil?
    Oh spit her forth forever, as your foe.
    Let the girl marry somebody in Hades.
    Since I have caught her in the open act,   655
    the only one in town who disobeyed,
    I shall not now proclaim myself a liar,
    but kill her. Let her sing her song of Zeus
    the guardian of blood kin.
    If I allow disorder in my house
    I'd surely have to license it abroad.   660
    A man who deals in fairness with his own,
    he can make manifest justice in the state.
    But he who crosses law, or forces it,
    or hopes to dictate orders to the rulers,
    shall never have a word of praise from me.   665
    The man the state has put in place must have

obedient hearing to his least command
when it is right, and even when it's not.
He who accepts this teaching I can trust,
ruler, or ruled, to function in his place,
to stand his ground even in the storm of spears,   670
a comrade to trust in battle at one's side.
There is no greater wrong than disobedience.
This ruins cities, this tears down our homes,
this breaks the battlefront in panic-rout.
If men live decently it is because
obedience saves their very lives for them.   675
So I must guard the men who yield to order,
not let myself be beaten by a woman.
Better, if it must happen, that a man
should overset me.
I won't be called weaker than womankind.   680

CHORUS LEADER
We think—unless our age is cheating us—
that what you say is sensible and right.

HAEMON
Father, the gods have given men good sense,
the highest and best possession that we have.
I couldn't find the words in which to claim   685
that there was error in your late remarks.
Yet someone else might bring some further light.
Because I am your son I must keep watch
on all men's doing where it touches you,
their speech, and most of all, their discontents.
Your presence frightens any common man   690
from saying things you would not care to hear.
But in dark corners I have heard them say
how the whole town is grieving for this girl,
unjustly doomed, if ever woman was,
to die in shame for glorious action done.   695
She would not leave her fallen, slaughtered brother

there, as he lay, unburied, for the birds
and hungry dogs to make an end of him.
Does she not truly deserve a golden prize?
This is the undercover speech in town.   700
       Father, your welfare is my greatest good.
What precious gift in life for any child
outweighs a father's fortune and good fame?
And so a father feels his children's faring.
So, do not have one mind, and one alone   705
that only your opinion can be right.
Whoever thinks that he alone is wise,
his eloquence, his mind, above the rest,
come the unfolding, it shows his emptiness.
A man, though wise, should never be ashamed   710
of learning more, and must not be too rigid.
Have you not seen the trees beside storm torrents—
the ones that bend preserve their limbs and leaves,
while the resistant perish root and branch?
And so the ship that will not slacken sail,   715
the ropes drawn tight, unyielding, overturns.
She ends the voyage with her keel on top.
No, yield your wrath, allow a change of stand.
Young as I am, if I may give advice,
I'd say it would be best if men were born   720
perfect in wisdom, but that failing this
(which often fails) it can be no dishonor
to learn from others when they speak good sense.

CHORUS LEADER

   Lord, if your son has spoken to the point
   you should take his lesson. He should do the same.   725
   Both sides have spoken well.

CREON

   At my age I'm to school my mind by his?
   This boy instructor is my master, then?

HAEMON

I urge no wrong. I'm young, but you should watch
my actions, not my years, to judge of me.

CREON

A loyal action, to respect disorder?   730

HAEMON

I wouldn't urge respect for wickedness.

CREON

You don't think she is sick with that disease?

HAEMON

Your fellow citizens maintain she's not.

CREON

Is the town to tell me how I ought to rule?

HAEMON

Now there you speak just like a boy yourself.   735

CREON

Am I to rule by other mind than mine?

HAEMON

No city is property of a single man.

CREON

But custom gives possession to the ruler.

HAEMON

You'd rule a desert beautifully alone.

CREON   *(To the Chorus.)*

It seems he's firmly on the woman's side.   740

HAEMON

If you're a woman. It is you I care for.

CREON

Wicked, to try conclusions with your father.

HAEMON

When you conclude unjustly, so I must.

CREON

Am I unjust, when I respect my office?

HAEMON

You don't respect it, trampling down the gods' due.   745

CREON

Your mind is poisoned. Weaker than a woman!

HAEMON

At least you'll never see me yield to shame.

CREON

Your whole long argument is but for her.

HAEMON

And you, and me, and for the gods below.

CREON

As long as she lives, you shall not marry her.   750

HAEMON

Then she shall die—and her death will bring another.

CREON

Your boldness makes more progress. Threats, indeed!

HAEMON

No threat, to speak against your empty plan.

CREON

Past due, sharp lessons for your empty brain.

HAEMON

If you weren't father, I should call you mad.   755

CREON

Don't flatter me with "father," you woman's slave.

HAEMON

You wish to speak but never wish to hear.

CREON

You think so? By Olympus, you shall not
revile me with these tauntings and go free.
Bring out the hateful creature; she shall die   760
full in his sight, close at her bridegroom's side.

HAEMON

Not at my side! Don't think that! She will not
die next to me. And you yourself will not
ever lay eyes upon my face again.
Find other friends to rave with after this.   765

(Exit Haemon, to the side.)

CHORUS LEADER

Lord, he has gone with all the speed of rage.
When such a young man is grieved his mind is hard.

CREON

Oh, let him go, and plan superhuman action.
In any case the girls shall not escape.

CHORUS LEADER

You plan the punishment of death for both?   770

CREON

Not her who did not do it. You are right.

CHORUS LEADER

And what death have you chosen for the other?

CREON

To take her where the foot of man comes not.
There shall I hide her in a hollowed cave
living, and leave her just so much to eat   775
as clears the city from the guilt of death.
There, if she prays to Death, the only god

of her respect, she may manage not to die.
Or she may learn at last, though much too late,
how honoring the dead is wasted labor.   780

                              (*Exit Creon into the palace.*)°

CHORUS [*singing*]

STROPHE

Love unconquered in fight, love who falls on our possessions:°
You rest at night in the soft bloom of a girl's face.
You cross the sea, you are known in the wildest lairs.   785
Not the immortal gods can escape you,
nor men of a day. Who has you within him is mad.   790

ANTISTROPHE

You twist the minds of the just. Wrong they pursue and are ruined.
You made this quarrel of kindred men before us now.
Desire looks clear from the eyes of a lovely bride: 795
power as strong as the founded world.
Aphrodite, goddess, is playing, with whom no man can fight.   800

              (*Antigone is brought from the palace under guard.*)

[*chanting*]

> Now I am carried beyond all bounds.
> My tears will not be checked.
> I see Antigone depart
> to the chamber where all must sleep.   805

ANTIGONE [*singing*]

STROPHE A

Men of my fathers' land, you see me go
my last journey. My last sight of the sun,
then never again. Death who brings all to sleep   810
takes me alive to the shore
of the river underground.
Not for me was the marriage hymn, nor will anyone start the song   815
at a wedding of mine. Acheron is my bridegroom.

CHORUS [*chanting*]

> With praise as your portion you go
> in fame to the vault of the dead.
> Untouched by wasting disease,
> not paying the price of the sword,   820
> of your own free will you go.
> Alone among mortals will you descend
> in life to the house of Death.

ANTIGONE [*singing*]

ANTISTROPHE A

Pitiful was the death that Phrygian stranger died,
our queen once, Tantalus' daughter. The rock by Sipylus   825
covered her over, like stubborn ivy it grew.
Still, as she wastes, the rain
and snow companion her, so men say.
Pouring down from her mourning eyes comes the water that
soaks the stone.   830
My own putting to sleep a god has arranged like hers.

CHORUS [*chanting*]

> God's child and god she was:
> but we are born to death.   835
> Yet even in death you will have your fame,
> to have gone like a god to your fate,
> in living and dying alike.

ANTIGONE [*singing*]

STROPHE B

Laughter against me now. In the name of our fathers' gods,
could you not wait till I went? Must affront be thrown in my face?   840
O city of wealthy men.
I call upon Dirce's spring,
I call upon Thebe's grove in the armored plain,   845
to be my witnesses, how with no friend's mourning,
by what decree I go to the fresh-made prison tomb.
Alive to the place of corpses, an alien still,   850
never at home with the living nor with the dead.

CHORUS

> You went to the furthest verge
> of daring, but there you tripped
> on the high pedestal of justice, and fell.   855
> Perhaps you are paying your father's pain.

ANTIGONE

ANTISTROPHE B

You speak of my darkest thought, my pitiful father's fame,
spread through all the world, and the doom that haunts our house,   860
the glorious house of Labdacus.
My mother's marriage bed.
Destruction where she lay with her husband-son,   865
my father. These are my parents and I their child.
I go to stay with them. My curse is to die unwed.
My brother, you found your fate when you found your bride,   870
you found it for me as well. Dead, you destroy my life.

CHORUS

> You showed respect for the dead.
> So we for you: but power
> is not to be thwarted so.
> Your self-willed temper has brought you down.   875

ANTIGONE

EPODE

Unwept, no wedding-song, unfriended, now I go
down the road made ready for me.
No longer am I allowed to see this holy light of the sun.   880
No friend bewails my fate.

(Creon enters from the palace.)°

CREON

When people sing the dirge for their own deaths
ahead of time, no one would ever stop
if they might hope that this would be of use.°
Take her away at once, and open up   885
the tomb I spoke of. Leave her there alone.

There let her choose: death, or a buried life.
No stain of guilt upon us in this case,
but she is exiled from our life on earth.   890

ANTIGONE
O tomb, O marriage chamber, hollowed-out
house that will watch forever, where I go—
to my own people, most of whom are there;
Persephone has taken them to her.
Last of them all, beyond the rest ill-fated,   895
I shall descend, before my course is run.
Still when I get there I may hope to find
I've come as a dear friend to my dear father,
to you, my mother, and my brother too.
All three of you have known my hand in death.   900
I washed your bodies, dressed them for the grave,
poured out the last libation at the tomb.
And now, Polyneices, you know the price I pay
for doing final service to your corpse.
    And yet the wise will know my choice was right.
Were I a mother, with children or husband dead,   905
I'd let them molder. I should not have chosen
in such a case to cross the state's decree.
What is the law that lies behind these words?
One husband gone, I might have found another,
or a child from a new man in the first child's place;   910
but with my parents covered up in death,
no brother for me, ever, could be born.
Such was the law by which I honored you.
But Creon thought the doing was a crime,   915
a dreadful daring, brother of my heart.
So now he takes and leads me out by force.
No marriage bed, no marriage song for me,
and since no wedding, so no child to rear.
I go, without a friend, struck down by fate,
living, to the hollow chambers of the dead.   920

What divine justice have I disobeyed?
Why, in my misery, look to the gods for help?
Can I call any of them my ally?
I stand convicted of impiety,
the evidence my pious duty done.
If the gods think that this is righteousness,   925
in suffering I'll see my error clear.
But if it is the others who are wrong
I wish them no greater punishment than mine.

CHORUS [*Chorus, Creon, and Antigone chanting in turn*]
The same tempest of mind
as ever, controls the girl.   930

CREON
Therefore her guards shall regret
the slowness with which they move.

ANTIGONE
That word comes close to death.

CREON
You are perfectly right in that;
I offer no grounds for hope.   935

ANTIGONE
O town of my fathers in Thebe's land,
O gods of our house!
I am led away and must not wait.
Look, leaders of Thebes,   940
I am last of your royal line.
Look what I suffer, at whose command,
because I respected the right.

(*Antigone is led away, to the side.*)

CHORUS [*singing*]
STROPHE A
Danaë suffered too.
She went from the light to the brass-built room,   945

bedchamber and tomb together. Like you, poor child,
she was of great descent, and more, she held and kept
the seed of the golden rain which was Zeus. 950
Fate has terrible power.
You cannot escape it by wealth or war.
No fort will keep it out, no ships outrun it.

ANTISTROPHE A

Remember the angry king, 955
son of Dryas, who raged against Dionysus and paid,
pent in a rock-walled prison. His bursting wrath
slowly went down. As the terror of madness went,
he learned of his frenzied attack on the god. 960
Fool, he had tried to stop
the dancing women possessed of god,
the fire of Bacchic rites, the songs and pipes. 965

STROPHE B

Where the dark rocks divide
sea from sea at the Bosporus,
is Thracian Salmydessus, where savage Ares 970
beheld the terrible blinding wounds
dealt to Phineus' sons by their father's wife. 975
Dark the eyes that looked to avenge their mother.
Sharp with her shuttle she struck, and blooded her hands.°

ANTISTROPHE B

Wasting they wept their fate,
settled when they were born 980
to Cleopatra, unhappy queen.
She was a princess too, of the ancient Erechthids,
but was reared in the cave of the wild North Wind, her father, 985
swift as a horse over the hills.
Half a goddess, still, child, she suffered like you.

(Enter, from the side, Teiresias, led by a boy attendant.)

TEIRESIAS
Elders of Thebes, we two have come one road,
two of us looking through one pair of eyes.
This is the way of walking for the blind.   990

CREON
Old Teiresias, what news has brought you here?

TEIRESIAS
I'll tell you. You in turn must trust the prophet.

CREON
I've always been attentive to your counsel.

TEIRESIAS
And therefore you have steered this city straight.

CREON
So I can say how helpful you have been.   995

TEIRESIAS
Again you are balanced on a razor's edge.

CREON
What is it? How I shudder at your words!

TEIRESIAS
You'll know, when you hear the signs that I have marked.
I sat where every bird of heaven comes   1000
in my old place of augury, and heard
bird cries I'd never known. They screeched about
goaded by madness, inarticulate.
I marked that they were tearing one another
with claws of murder. I could hear the wing-beats.
I was afraid, so straightaway I tried   1005
burnt sacrifice upon the flaming altar.
No fire caught my offerings. Slimy ooze
dripped on the ashes, smoked and sputtered there.
Gall burst its bladder, vanished into vapor;   1010

the fat dripped from the bones and would not burn.
These are the omens of the rites that failed,
as this boy here has told me. He's my guide
as I am guide to others.
Why has this sickness struck against the state?   1015
Through your decision.
All of the altars of the town are choked
with leavings of the dogs and birds; their feast
was on that fated, fallen son of Oedipus.
So the gods accept no offering from us,
not prayer, nor flame of sacrifice. The birds   1020
cry out a sound that I cannot distinguish,
gorged with the greasy blood of that dead man.

      Think of these things, my son. All men may err,
but error once committed, he's no fool
nor unsuccessful, who can change his mind   1025
and cure the trouble he has fallen in.
Stubbornness and stupidity are twins.
Yield to the dead. Why goad him where he lies?
What use to kill the dead a second time?   1030
I speak for your own good. And I am right.
Learning from a wise counselor is not pain
if what he speaks are profitable words.

CREON

Old man, you all, like bowmen at a mark,
have bent your bows at me. I've had my share
of seers: I've been an item in your accounts.   1035
Make profit, trade in Lydian electrum,
pure gold of India; that's your chief desire.
But you will never cover up that corpse,
not if the very eagles tear their food   1040
from him, and leave it at the throne of Zeus.
I wouldn't give him up for burial
in fear of that pollution. For I know

no mortal being can pollute the gods.
Yes, old Teiresias, human beings fall;   1045
the clever ones the furthest, when they plead
a shameful case so well in hope of profit.

TEIRESIAS

Alas!
What man can tell me, has he thought at all . . .

CREON

What tired cliché's coming from your lips?

TEIRESIAS

How the best of all possessions is good counsel.   1050

CREON

And so is foolishness the worst of all.

TEIRESIAS

But you're infected with that same disease.

CREON

I'm reluctant to be uncivil to a seer . . .

TEIRESIAS

You're that already. You have said I lie.

CREON

Well, the whole crew of seers are money-mad.   1055

TEIRESIAS

And the whole tribe of tyrants grab at gain.

CREON

Do you realize you are talking to a king?

TEIRESIAS

I know. Who helped you save this town you hold?

CREON

You're a wise seer, but you love wickedness.

TEIRESIAS

You'll bring me to speak the unspeakable, very soon.   1060

CREON

Well, speak it out. But do not speak for profit.

TEIRESIAS

Do I seem to have spoken for profit, with regard to you?

CREON

Know this, that you can't buy and sell my policies.

TEIRESIAS

Know well yourself, the sun won't roll its course   1065
many more days, before you come to give
corpse for these corpses, child of your own loins.
For you've confused the upper and lower worlds.
You settled a living person without honor
in a tomb; you keep up here that which belongs   1070
below, a corpse unburied and unholy.
Not you, nor any god on high should have
any business with this. The violation's yours.
So the patient, foul punishers lie in wait
to track you down: the Furies sent by Hades   1075
and by all gods will even you with your victims.
Now say that I am bribed! The time is close
when men and women shall wail within your house,
and all the cities that you fought in war°   1080
whose sons had burial from wild beasts, or dogs,
or birds that brought the stench of your great wrong
back to each hearth, they all will move against you.
A bowman, as you said, I send my shafts,   1085
since you provoked me, straight. You'll feel the wound.
      Boy, take me home now. Let him spend his rage
on younger men, and learn to calm his tongue,
and keep a better mind than now he does.   1090

(Exit, to the side.)

CHORUS LEADER
Lord, he has gone. Terrible prophecies!
And since the time my hair turned gray from black,
his sayings to the city have been true.

CREON
I also know this. And my mind is torn.   1095
To yield is dreadful. But to stand against him,
and shatter my spirit in doom is dreadful too.

CHORUS LEADER
Now you must seek good counsel, and take advice.

CREON
What must I do? Speak, and I shall obey.

CHORUS LEADER
Go free the maiden from that rocky house;   1100
and bury the dead who lies in readiness.

CREON
This is your counsel? You would have me yield?

CHORUS LEADER
Quick as you can. The gods move very fast
when they bring ruin on misguided men.

CREON
How hard, abandonment of my desire!   1105
But I can fight necessity no more.

CHORUS LEADER
Do it yourself. Leave it to no one else.

CREON
I'll go at once. Come, followers, to your work.
You that are here round up the other fellows.
Take axes with you, hurry to that place
that overlooks us there.   1110
And I, since my decision's overturned,

the one who bound her will set her free myself.
I've come to fear it's best to hold the laws
of old tradition to the end of life.

(Exit, to the side.)

CHORUS [*singing*]

STROPHE A

God of the many names, Semele's proud delight,   1115
child of Olympian thunder, Italy's master,
lord of Eleusis, where all men come   1120
to Mother Demeter's plain:
Bacchus, who dwell in Thebes,
by Ismenus' running water,
where wild Bacchic women are at home,
on the soil of the dragon seed.   1125

ANTISTROPHE A

Seen in the glaring flame, high on the double crags,
with the nymphs of Parnassus at play on the hill,
seen by Castalia's fresh fountain: 1130
you come from the ivied heights
and the green grape-filled coast of Euboea.
In immortal words they cry
your name, lord, who watch the roads,   1135
the many streets of Thebes.

STROPHE B

This is your city, honored beyond the rest,
the town of your mother's miracle-death.
Now, as we wrestle with grim disease,   1140
come with healing step along Parnassus' slope
or over the resounding sea.   1145

ANTISTROPHE B

Leader in dance of the fire-pulsing stars,
overseer of the voices of night,
child of Zeus, be manifest,

with due companionship of maenads dancing 1150
and honoring their lord, Iacchus.

(Enter Messenger, from the side.)

MESSENGER

Neighbors of Cadmus, and Amphion's house, 1155
there is no kind of state in human life
which I would now dare either praise or blame.
Fortune sets straight, and Fortune overturns
the happy or unhappy, day by day.
No prophecy can deal with men's affairs. 1160
Creon was envied once, as I believe,
for having saved this city from its foes
and having got full power in this land.
He steered it well. And he had noble sons.
Now everything is gone. 1165
Yes, when a man has lost all happiness,
he's not alive. Call him a breathing corpse.
Be very rich at home. Live as a king.
But once your joy has gone, though these are left
they are smoke's shadow to lost happiness. 1170

CHORUS LEADER

What is the grief of princes that you bring?

MESSENGER

They're dead. The living are responsible.

CHORUS LEADER

Who died? Who did the murder? Tell us now.

MESSENGER

Haemon is gone. His own flesh and blood did him in. 1175

CHORUS LEADER

But whose arm struck? His father's or his own?

MESSENGER

He killed himself, angry at his father's killing.

CHORUS LEADER

Seer, all too true the prophecy you told!

MESSENGER

This is the state of things. Now make your plans.

(Enter Eurydice, from the palace.)

CHORUS LEADER

Eurydice is with us now, I see.   1180
Creon's poor wife. She may have come by chance.
She may have heard something about her son.

EURYDICE

I heard your talk as I was coming out
to greet the goddess Pallas with my prayer.   1185
And as I moved the bolts that held the door
I heard the voice of family disaster.
I fell back fainting in my women's arms.
But say again, just what is the news you bring.   1190
I, whom you speak to, have known grief before.

MESSENGER

Dear lady, I was there, and I shall tell,
leaving out nothing of the true account.
Why should I make it soft for you with tales
to prove myself a liar? Truth is right.   1195
I followed your husband to the plain's far edge,
where Polyneices' corpse was lying still
unpitied. The dogs had torn him all apart.
We prayed the goddess of all journeyings,
and Pluto, that they turn their wrath to kindness;   1200
we gave the final purifying bath,
then burned the poor remains on new-cut boughs,
and heaped a high mound of his native earth.
Then turned we to the maiden's rocky bed,
approaching Hades' hollow marriage chamber.   1205
But, still far off, one of us heard a voice
in keen lament by that unblest abode.

He ran and told the master. As Creon came
he heard confusion crying. He groaned and spoke: 1210
"Am I a prophet now, and do I tread
the saddest of all roads I ever trod?
My son's voice crying! Servants, run up close,
stand by the tomb and look, push through the crevice   1215
where we built the pile of rock, right to the entry.
Find out if that is Haemon's voice I hear
or if the gods are tricking me indeed."
We obeyed the order of our mournful master.
In the far corner of the tomb we saw   1220
her, hanging by the neck, caught in a noose
of her own linen veiling.
Haemon embraced her as she hung, and mourned
his bride's destruction, dead and gone below,
his father's actions, the unfated marriage.   1225
When Creon saw him, he groaned terribly,
and went toward him, and called him with lament:
"What have you done, what did you have in mind,
what happened so as thus to ruin you?
Come out, my child, I do beseech you, come!"   1230
The boy looked at him with his angry eyes,
spat in his face and spoke no further word.
He drew his sword, but as his father ran,
he missed his aim. Then the unhappy boy,
in anger at himself, leant on the blade: 1235
it entered, half its length, into his side.
While he was conscious he embraced the maiden,
holding her gently. Last, he gasped out blood,
red blood on her white cheek.
Corpse on a corpse he lies. He found his marriage,   1240
its celebration in the halls of Hades.
So he has made it very clear to men
that to reject good counsel is a crime.

(*Exit Eurydice, back into the palace.*)

CHORUS LEADER

What do you make of this? The queen has gone
in silence, with no word of evil or of good.   1245

MESSENGER

I wonder at her, too. But we can hope
that she has gone to mourn her son within
with her own women, not before the town.
She knows discretion. She will do no wrong.   1250

CHORUS LEADER

I am not sure. This muteness may portend
as great disaster as a loud lament.

MESSENGER

I will go in and see if some deep plan
hides in her heart's wild pain. You may be right.   1255
There can be heavy danger in mute grief.

(Exit the Messenger into the palace. Creon enters from the side
with his followers. They are carrying Haemon's body on a bier.)

CHORUS [chanting]

But look, the king draws near.
His own hand brings
the witness of his crime,
the doom he brought on himself.   1260

CREON [singing in what follows, while the Chorus and Messenger speak]

STROPHE A

O crimes of my wicked heart,
harshness bringing death.
You see the killer, you see the kin he killed.
My planning was all unblest.   1265
Son, you have died too soon.
Oh, you have gone away
through my fault, not your own.

CHORUS LEADER

You have learned justice, though it comes too late.   1270

CREON

Yes, I have learned in sorrow. It was a god who struck,
who has weighted my head with disaster; he drove me to wild
    strange ways,
his heavy heel on my joy. 1275
Oh sorrows, sorrows of men.

(Reenter the Messenger, from the palace.)

MESSENGER

Master, you hold one sorrow in your hands
but you have more, stored up inside the house. 1280

CREON

What further suffering can come on me?

MESSENGER

Your wife has died. The dead man's mother indeed,
poor soul, with wounds freshly inflicted.

CREON

ANTISTROPHE A

Hades, harbor of all,
you have destroyed me now. 1285
Terrible news to hear, horror the tale you tell.
I was dead, and you kill me again.
Boy, did I hear you right? 1290
Did you say the queen was dead,
slaughter on slaughter heaped?

(The central doors of the palace open, and
the corpse of Eurydice is revealed.)

CHORUS LEADER

Now you can see. Concealment is all over.

CREON

My second sorrow is here. Surely no fate remains 1295
which can strike me again. Just now, I held my son in my arms.
And now I see her dead.
Woe for the mother and son. 1300

MESSENGER

There, by the altar, dying on the sword,°
her eyes fell shut. She wept her older son,
Megareus, who died before, and this one. Finally
she cursed you as the killer of her children.   1305

CREON

STROPHE B

I am mad with fear. Will no one strike
and kill me with cutting sword?
Sorrowful, soaked in sorrow to the bone!   1310

MESSENGER

Yes, for she held you guilty in the death
of him before you, and the elder dead.

CREON

How did she die?

MESSENGER

Struck home at her own heart   1315
when she had heard of Haemon's suffering.

CREON

This is my guilt, all mine. I killed you, I say it clear.
Servants, take me away, out of the sight of men.   1320
I who am nothing more than nothing now.   1325

CHORUS LEADER

Your plan is good—if any good is left.
Best to cut short our sorrow.

CREON

ANTISTROPHE B

Let me go, let me go. May death come quick,
bringing my final day!   1330
O let me never see tomorrow's dawn.

CHORUS LEADER

That is the future's. We must look to now.
What will be is in other hands than ours.   1335

CREON

All my desire was in that prayer of mine.

CHORUS LEADER

Pray not again. No mortal can escape
the doom prepared for him.

CREON [*singing*]

Take me away at once, the frantic man who killed   1340
my son, against my meaning, and you too, my wife.
I cannot look at either, I cannot rest.
My life is warped past cure. Fate unbearable   1345
has leapt down on my head.

(Creon and his attendants enter the palace.)

CHORUS [*chanting*]

Our happiness depends
on wisdom all the way.
The gods must have their due.
Great words by men of pride   1350
bring greater blows upon them.
So wisdom comes to the old.

HIPPOLYTUS

EURIPIDES
Translated by David Grene

INTRODUCTION TO EURIPIDES' HIPPOLYTUS

Euripides presented *Hippolytus* in 428 BCE and won first prize. It is, however, a second version; a previous *Hippolytus* (lost) had been considered scandalous and was badly received. Sophocles used the same story in his *Phaedra*. This is lost, and there is no clue to its date. Seneca in his *Phaedra*, Jean Racine in his *Phèdre*, and Eugene O'Neill in his *Desire under the Elms* have, in their own ways, also retold the story.

Theseus, king of Athens, had an illegitimate son, Hippolytus, by an Amazon mother. Late in life Theseus married a young woman, Phaedra, princess of Crete, who bore him two sons. Phaedra fell in love with Hippolytus, and her desire was communicated to him. He rejected it in horror, and Phaedra (in this version, by means of a suicide note) informed Theseus that Hippolytus had raped her; she then killed herself. Theseus caused his son's death by praying to his own father, Poseidon, to destroy him. But Artemis finally revealed the truth and established a hero cult of Hippolytus in his honor.

This story of the young man tempted and traduced has many parallels in Greek legend, and also in the biblical story of Joseph and the wife of Potiphar. The parallels, however, involve the prompt vindication of the hero and launch him on a career of heroic exploits. The women in these cases figure only as temptresses. Euripides by contrast has gone with great sympathy into the feelings of Phaedra, a helpless victim of Aphrodite whose mind clings despite all to its integrity. Hippolytus too, with his peculiar devotion to Artemis and his own virginal purity, constitutes a unique model of a Greek hero.

HIPPOLYTUS

Characters   THESEUS, king of Athens
                HIPPOLYTUS, his son by the queen of
                the Amazons
                PHAEDRA, Theseus' wife, stepmother to
                Hippolytus
                A SERVANT
                A MESSENGER°
                THE NURSE
                CHORUS OF WOMEN of Troezen
                A CHORUS OF HUNTSMEN, in attendance
                on Hippolytus
                APHRODITE
                ARTEMIS

Scene: Troezen, in front of the house of Theseus. In front of the house
there are two statues, one of Artemis and one of Aphrodite.

(Enter Aphrodite.)

APHRODITE
    I am called the Goddess Cypris:
    I am mighty among men and they honor me by many names.
    Of all who live and see the light of sun
    from Atlas' pillars to the tide of Pontus,
    those who worship my power in all humility
    I exalt in honor.   5
    But those whose pride is stiff-necked against me
    I lay by the heels.

There is joy in the heart of a god also
when honored by men.
   Now I will quickly tell you the truth of this story.
Hippolytus, son of Theseus by the Amazon,   10
pupil of holy Pittheus,
alone among the folk of this land of Troezen has
   blasphemed me
counting me vilest of the gods in heaven.
He will none of the bed of love nor marriage,
but honors Apollo's sister, Artemis, Zeus' daughter,   15
counting her greatest of all divinities.
He is with her continually, this maiden goddess, in the
   greenwood.
He hunts with swift hounds and clears the land of wild beasts,
sharing in greater than mortal companionship.
I do not grudge him such privileges: why should I?   20
But for the wrongs that he has done to me
I shall punish Hippolytus this day.
I have no need to toil to win my end:
much of the task has been already done.
He came once from Pittheus' house to the country of Pandion
that he might see and be initiate in the holy mysteries.   25
Phaedra, his father's noble wife, saw him
and her heart was filled with the longings of dreadful love.
This was my work.
So before ever she came to this land of Troezen
close to the rock of Pallas that looks across to it,   30
she dedicated a temple to Cypris,
for her love dwells in a foreign land.
Ages to come will call this temple after him,
the temple of the Goddess Near Hippolytus.
When Theseus left the land of Cecrops,
flying from the guilty stain of the murder of the Pallantids,   35
condemning himself to a year's exile
he sailed with his wife to this land.
Here she groans in bitterness of heart

and the goads of love prick her cruelly,
and she is like to die—in silence,
and none of the servants know of her sickness.   40
But her love is not to end up that way.
I will reveal the matter to Theseus and all shall come out.
Father shall slay son with curses—
this son that is hateful to me.
For once lord Poseidon, the ruler of the sea,
granted this favor to Theseus,   45
that three of his prayers to the god would find answer.
Renowned shall Phaedra be in her death, but none the less
die she must.
Her suffering shall not weigh in the scale so much
that I should let my enemies go untouched
escaping payment of a retribution
sufficient to satisfy me.   50
    Look, here is the son of Theseus, Hippolytus!
He has just left the toils of his hunting.
I will leave this place.
See the great crowd of servants that throngs upon his heels
and sings the praise of Artemis in hymns!   55
He does not know
that the doors of death are open for him,
that he is looking on his last sun.

        (Exit Aphrodite. Enter Hippolytus from the side, attended by a
        Chorus of friends and servants carrying hunting implements.)

HIPPOLYTUS [singing]
    Follow me, follow me singing
    of Artemis,
    heavenly one, child of Zeus,
    Artemis!
    We are the wards of your care.   60

CHORUS OF HUNTSMEN [singing]
    Hail, mistress and queen, holiest one!

Hail, daughter of Zeus!
Hail, Artemis, maiden Daughter of Zeus and Leto!
Most beautiful of virgins by far!   65
Dweller in the spacious sky,
in the palace of your noble father,
in Zeus' golden glistening house!
Hail!
Maiden goddess most beautiful, most beautiful of all those who
*   live in Olympus!*   70

(*Hippolytus lays a garland on the statue of Artemis.*)

HIPPOLYTUS

My sovereign lady, I bring you ready woven
this garland. It was I that plucked and wove it,
plucked it for you in your inviolate meadow.
No shepherd dares to feed his flock within it;   75
no reaper plies a busy scythe within it:
only the bees in springtime haunt the inviolate meadow.
Its gardener is the spirit Reverence who
refreshes it with water from the river.
Not those who by instruction have profited
to learn, but in whose very soul the seed   80
of purity and self-control toward
all things alike Nature has deeply rooted,
they alone may gather flowers there! The others,
the impure, may not.
    Loved Mistress, here I offer you this coronal;
it is a true worshipper's hand that gives it you
to crown the golden glory of your hair.
With no man else I share this privilege
that I am with you and to your words   85
can answer words. True, I may only hear:
I may not see you face to face.
So may I turn the post set at life's end
even as I began the race.

SERVANT

King—for I will not call you "Master," that belongs
to the gods only—will you take good advice?

HIPPOLYTUS

Certainly I will. I would not want to seem a fool.   90

SERVANT

In men's communities one rule holds good,
do you know it, King?

HIPPOLYTUS

                              Not I. What is this rule?

SERVANT

Men hate the haughty of heart who will not be
the friend of every man.

HIPPOLYTUS

                              And rightly too:
For a haughty heart breeds odium among men.

SERVANT

And affability wins favor, then?   95

HIPPOLYTUS

Abundant favor. Yes, and profit, too,
at little cost of inconvenience.

SERVANT

Do you think that it's the same among the gods?

HIPPOLYTUS

If we in our world and the gods in theirs
know the same usages—yes.

SERVANT

                              Then, King, how comes it
that for a venerable goddess you have not even
a word of salutation?

HIPPOLYTUS

Which goddess?
Be careful, or you will find that tongue of yours   100
may make a serious mistake.

SERVANT

This goddess here
who stands before your gates, the goddess Cypris.°

HIPPOLYTUS

I worship her—but from a long way off,
for I am pure.

SERVANT

Yet she's a venerable goddess,
and great is her renown throughout the world.

HIPPOLYTUS

Men make their choice: one man honors one god,°
and one another.

SERVANT

Well, good fortune guard you,
if you have as much good sense as you should have.   105

HIPPOLYTUS

A god of nocturnal prowess is not my god.

SERVANT

The honors of the gods you must not scant, my son.

HIPPOLYTUS

Go, men, into the house and look to supper.
A plentiful table is an excellent thing
after the hunt. And you

(Singling some out.)

rub down my horses.   110
When I have eaten I shall set them in the yoke and exercise
    them as is suitable.
As for your Cypris here—a long good-bye to her!

(Exit Hippolytus into the house accompanied by
the Chorus, except for the old Servant.)

SERVANT

O sovereign Cypris, we must not imitate
the young men when they have such thoughts as these.
As fits a slave to speak, here at your image   115
I pray and worship. You should be forgiving
when one that has a young tempestuous heart
speaks foolish words. Seem not to hear them.
You should be wiser than mortals, being gods.   120

(Exit the Servant. Enter Chorus of women of Troezen.)

CHORUS [*singing*]

STROPHE A

There is a rock streaming with water,
whose source, men say, is Ocean,
and it pours from the heart of its stone a spring
where pitchers may dip and be filled.
My friend was there and in the river water   125
she dipped and washed the royal purple robes,
and spread them on the rock's warm back
where the sunbeams played.
It was from her I heard at first
of the news of my mistress' sorrow.   130

ANTISTROPHE A

She lies on her bed within the house
and fever wracks her,
and she hides her golden head in finespun robes.
This is the third day   135
she has eaten no bread
and her body is pure and fasting.
For she would willingly bring her life to anchor
at the end of its voyage
in the gloomy harbor of death.   140

Is it Pan's frenzy that possesses you
or is Hecate's madness upon you, maid?
Can it be the holy Corybants,
or the Mighty Mother who rules the mountains?
Are you wasted in suffering thus   145
for a sin against Dictynna, queen of hunters?
Are you perhaps unhallowed, having offered
no sacrifice to her from taken victims?
For she goes through the waters of Limnae
and can travel on dry land beyond the sea,
the eddying salt sea.   150

ANTISTROPHE B

Can it be that some other woman's love,
a secret love that hides itself from you,
has beguiled your husband,
the sovereign lord of Erechtheus'
people, that prince of noble birth?
Or has some sailor from the shores of Crete   155
put in at this harbor hospitable to sailors,
bearing a message for our queen,
and so because he told her some calamity
her spirit is bound in chains of grief
and she lies on her bed in sorrow?   160

EPODE

Unhappy is the compound of woman's nature;
the torturing misery of helplessness,
the helplessness of childbirth and its madness,
are linked to it forever.
My body, too, has felt this thrill of pain,   165
and I called on Artemis, queen of the bow;
she has my reverence always
as she goes in the company of the gods.

[chanting]

But here is the old woman, the queen's nurse,   170
here at the door. She is bringing her mistress out.
There is a gathering cloud upon her face.
What is the matter? My soul is eager to know.
What can have made the queen so pale?
What can have wasted her body so?   175

(Enter the Nurse from the house, supporting Phaedra.)

NURSE [chanting, while Phaedra sings]
A weary thing is sickness and its pains!
What must I do now? What should I leave undone?
Here is light and air, the brightness of the sky.
I have brought out the couch on which you tossed
in fever—here, clear of the house.   180
Your every word has been to bring you out,
but when you're here, you hurry in again.
You find no constant pleasure anywhere
for when your joy is upon you, suddenly
you're foiled and cheated.
There's no content for you in what you have
for you're forever finding something dearer,
some other thing—because you have it not.   185
It's better to be sick than nurse the sick.
Sickness is single trouble for the sufferer:
but nursing means vexation of the mind,
and hard work for the hands besides.
The life of humankind is complete misery:
we find no resting place from calamity.   190
But something other dearer still than life°
the darkness hides and mist encompasses;
we are proved luckless lovers of this thing
that glitters in our world: no man
can tell us of that other life, expounding   195
what is under the earth: we know nothing of it.
Idly we drift, on idle stories carried.

PHAEDRA   (To the servants.)

    Lift me up! Lift my head up! All the muscles
    are slack and useless. Here, you, take my hands.
    They're beautiful, my hands and arms!   200
    Take away this headdress! It is too heavy to wear.
    Take it away! Let my hair fall free on my shoulders.

NURSE

    Quiet, child, quiet! Do not so restlessly
    keep tossing to and fro! It's easier
    to bear an illness if you have some patience   205
    and the spirit of good breeding.
    We all must suffer sometimes: we are mortal.

PHAEDRA

    Oh,
    if I could only draw from the dewy spring
    a draught of fresh pure water!
    If I could only lie beneath the poplars,   210
    in the tufted meadow and find my rest there!

NURSE

    Child, why do you rave so? There are others here.
    Cease tossing out these wild demented words
    whose driver is madness.

PHAEDRA

    Bring me to the mountains! I will go to the mountains,   215
    among the pine trees where the huntsmen's pack
    trails spotted stags and hangs upon their heels.
    By the gods, how I long to set the hounds on, shouting,
    and poise the Thessalian javelin drawing it back—
    here where my fair hair hangs above the ear—   220
    I would hold in my hand a spear with a steel point.

NURSE

    What ails you, child? What is this love of hunting,
    and you a lady! Draught of fresh spring water?

Here, beside the tower there is a sloping ridge   225
with springs enough to satisfy your thirst.

PHAEDRA

Artemis, mistress of the Salty Lake,
mistress of the ring echoing to the racers' hoofs,
if only I could gallop your level stretches,   230
and break Venetian colts!

NURSE

This is sheer madness again,
that prompts such whirling, frenzied, senseless words.
Here at one moment you're afire with longing
to hunt wild beasts and you'd go to the hills,
and then again all your desire is horses,
horses on the sands beyond the reach of the breakers.   235
Indeed, it would need a mighty prophet, my child,
to tell which of the gods it is that
jerks you from your true course and thwarts your wits!

PHAEDRA [chanting]

O, I am miserable! What is this I've done?
Where have I strayed from the highway of good sense?   240
I was mad. It was the madness sent from some god
that made me fall.
I am unhappy, so unhappy! Nurse,
cover my face again. I am ashamed   245
of what I said. Cover me up. The tears
are flowing, and my face is turned to shame.
Having my mind straight is bitterness to my heart;
yet madness is terrible. It is better then
that I should die and know no more of anything.

NURSE [chanting]

There, now, you are covered up. But my own body: 250
when will death cover that? I have learned much
from my long life. The mixing bowl of friendship,

the love of one for the other, must be tempered.
Fondness must not touch the marrow of the soul.   255
Our affections must be breakable chains, that we
can cast them off or tighten them.
That one soul so for two should be in travail
as I for her, that is a heavy burden.   260
The ways of life that are most unbending
trip us up more, they say, than bring us joy.
They're enemies to health. So I praise less
the extreme than temperance in everything.   265
The wise will agree with me.

CHORUS LEADER
Old woman, you are Phaedra's faithful nurse.
We can see that the queen is in trouble, but the cause
that ails her is black mystery to us.
We would like to hear you tell us what is the matter.   270

NURSE [*speaking*]
I have asked and know no more. She will not tell me.

CHORUS LEADER
Not even what began it?

NURSE
                          And my answer
is still the same: of all this she will not speak.

CHORUS LEADER
But see how ill she is, and how her body
is wracked and wasted!

NURSE
                    Yes, she has eaten nothing
for two days now.   275

CHORUS LEADER
                 Is this the scourge of madness?
Or can it be . . . that dying is what she seeks?

NURSE

Dying? Well, she is starving herself to death.

CHORUS LEADER

I wonder that her husband allows this.

NURSE

She hides her troubles, says that she isn't sick.

CHORUS LEADER

But does he not look into her face and see   280
a witness that disproves her?

NURSE

                                    No, he is gone.
He is away from home, in foreign lands.

CHORUS LEADER

Why, you must force her then, to find the cause
of this mind-wandering sickness!

NURSE

                                    Every means
I have tried and still have won no foot of ground.
But I'll not give up trying, even now.   285
You are here and can in person bear me witness
that I am loyal to my masters always,
even in misfortune's hour.
    Dear child, let us both forget our former words.
Be kinder, you: unknit that ugly frown
and track of thought. And as for me, I'll leave   290
that point I could not follow you at: I'll take
another and a better argument.
    If you are sick and it is some unmentionable malady,
here are women standing at your side to help.
But if your troubles may be told to men,   295
speak, that a doctor may pronounce upon it.
So, not a word! Oh, why will you not speak?
There is no remedy in silence, child.

Either I am wrong and then you should correct me;
or right, and you should yield to what I say.
Say something! Look at me!   300
    Women, I have tried and tried and all for nothing.
We are as far as ever from our goal.
It was the same before—she was not melted
by anything I said, and now she still won't listen.
    But this you shall know, though to my reasoning
you are more dumbly obstinate than the sea:
If you die, you will be a traitor to your children.   305
They will never know their share in a father's palace.
No, by the Amazon queen, the mighty rider
who bore a master for your children,
one bastard in birth but trueborn son in mind,
you know him well—Hippolytus . . .

PHAEDRA
  Ah!

NURSE
  So that has touched you?   310

PHAEDRA
  You have killed me, nurse. For the gods' sake, I entreat you,
  never again speak about that man to me.

NURSE
  You see? You have come to your senses, yet despite that,
  you will not make your children happy nor
  save your own life besides.

PHAEDRA
  I love my children.
  It's another storm of fortune that batters me.   315

NURSE
  There is no stain of blood upon your hands?

PHAEDRA

My hands are clean: the stain is in my heart.

NURSE

The hurt comes from outside? Some enemy?

PHAEDRA

One I love destroys me. Neither of us wills it.

NURSE

Has Theseus done some wrong against you then?   320

PHAEDRA

May I be equally guiltless in his sight!

NURSE

What is this terror urging you to death?

PHAEDRA

Leave me to do wrong. My wrongs are not against you.

NURSE

Not of my will, but yours, you'll cast me off.

PHAEDRA

Are you trying to force me, clasping my hand as suppliant?   325

NURSE

Your knees too—and I never will let you go.

PHAEDRA

Sorrow, nurse, sorrow for you, if you find out.

NURSE

Can I know greater sorrow than losing you?

PHAEDRA

It will kill you. But for me, honor lies in silence.

NURSE

And yet you hide it, though I plead for what's good?   330

PHAEDRA

Yes, for I seek to win good out of shame.

NURSE

But won't you earn more honor if you speak?

PHAEDRA

By the gods, let go my hand and go away!

NURSE

No, for you have not given me what you must.

PHAEDRA

I yield. Your suppliant hand compels my reverence.　　　　335

NURSE

I will say no more. Yours is the word from now.

PHAEDRA

Unhappy mother, what a love was yours!

NURSE

It is her love for the bull you mean, dear child?

PHAEDRA

Unhappy sister, bride of Dionysus!

NURSE

Why these ill-boding words about your kin?　　　　340

PHAEDRA

And I the unlucky third, see how I end!

NURSE

Your words are wounds. Where will your tale conclude?

PHAEDRA

Mine is an inherited curse. It is not new.

NURSE

I have not yet heard what I most want to know.

PHAEDRA

Ah!
If you could say for me what I must say myself.   345

NURSE

I am no prophet to know your hidden secrets.

PHAEDRA

What does it mean to say someone's in love?

NURSE

Sweetest and bitterest, both in one, at once.

PHAEDRA

One of those two, I've known, and all too well.

NURSE

Are you in love, my child? And who is he?   350

PHAEDRA

There is a man . . . his mother was an Amazon . . .

NURSE

You mean Hippolytus?

PHAEDRA

                                   You
have spoken it, not I.

NURSE

What do you mean? This is my death.
Women, this is past bearing. I'll not bear
life after this. A curse upon the daylight!
A curse upon this shining sun above us!   355
I'll throw myself from a cliff, throw myself headlong!
I'll be rid of life somehow, I'll die somehow!
Farewell to all of you! This is the end for me.
     Chaste and temperate people—not of their own will—
fall in love, badly. Cypris, you are no god.

You are something stronger than a god if that can be.   360
You have ruined her and me and all this house.

(Exit the Nurse.)

CHORUS [*singing*]

STROPHE

Did you hear, did you hear
the queen crying aloud,
telling of a calamity
which no ear should hear?
I would rather die
than think such thoughts as yours.   365
I am sorry for your trouble.
Alas for troubles, man-besetting.
You are dead, you yourself
have dragged your ruin to the light.
What can happen now in the long
dragging stretch of the rest of your days?
Some new thing will befall the house.   370
We know now, we know now
how your love will end,
poor unhappy Cretan girl!

PHAEDRA

Hear me, you women of Troezen who live
in this extremity of land, this anteroom to Argos.
Many a time in night's long empty spaces   375
I have pondered on the causes of a life's shipwreck.
I think that our lives are worse than the mind's quality
would warrant. There are many who know good sense.
But look. We know the good, we see it clear.   380
But we can't bring it to achievement. Some
are betrayed by their own laziness, and others
value some other pleasure above virtue.
There are so many pleasures in this life—
long gossiping talks and leisure, that sweet curse.

Then there is shame that thwarts us. Shame is of two kinds.   385
The one is harmless, but the other's a plague.
For clarity's sake, we should not talk of "shame,"
a single word for two quite different things.
These then are my views. Nothing can now seduce me   390
to the opposite opinion. I will tell you
in my own case the track which my mind followed.
    At first when love had struck me, I reflected
how best to bear it. Silence was my first plan:
to conceal that illness. For I knew the tongue
is not to be trusted: it can criticize   395
another's faulty thoughts, but on its owner
it brings a thousand troubles.
    Next, I believed that I could conquer love,
conquer it with discretion and good sense.
And when that too failed me, I resolved to die.   400
And death is the best plan. No one will dispute that.
I want to have my virtues known and honored—
not many witnesses when I do something wrong!
I know what is involved: I know the scandal;   405
and all too well I know that I am a woman,
object of hate to all. Destruction light
upon the wife who first did shame her bed
by dalliance with strangers. In the wives   410
of noble houses first this taint began:
when wickedness approves itself to those
of noble birth, it will surely be approved
by their inferiors. Truly, too, I hate
lip-worshippers of purity and temperance, who
own lecherous daring when they have privacy.
O Cypris, sea-born goddess, how can they   415
look frankly in the faces of their husbands
and never shiver with fear lest their accomplice,
the darkness and the rafters of the house,
take voice and cry aloud?
This then, my friends, is my destruction:

I cannot bear that I should be discovered   420
a traitor to my husband and my children.
God grant them rich and glorious life in Athens—
famous Athens—freedom in word and deed,
and from their mother an honorable name.
It makes the stoutest-hearted man a slave
if in his soul he knows his parents' shame.   425
The proverb runs: "There is one thing alone
that stands comparison with life in value,
a quiet conscience," . . . a just and quiet conscience
for whoever can attain it.
Time holds a mirror, as for a young girl,
and sometimes as occasion falls, it shows us
the evildoers of the world. I would not wish
that I should be seen among them.   430

CHORUS LEADER
How virtue is held lovely everywhere,
and harvests a good name among mankind!

(Enter the Nurse again.)

NURSE
Mistress, the trouble you told me just now,
coming on me so suddenly, frightened me;
but now I realize that I was foolish.   435
In this world second thoughts, it seems, are best.
Your case is not so extraordinary,
beyond thought or reason. The goddess in her anger
has smitten you, and you are in love. What wonder
is this? There are many thousands suffer with you.
So, you will die for love? And all the others,   440
who love, and who will love, must they die, too?
How will that profit them? The tide of Cypris,
at its full surge, is not withstandable.
Upon the yielding spirit she comes gently,

but if she finds one arrogant and superior   445
she seizes him and abuses him completely.
Cypris wings her way through the air; she is in the sea,
in its foaming billows; from her everything
that is, is born. For she engenders us
and sows the seed of desire whereof we're born,   450
all we her children, living on the earth.
He who has read the writings of the ancients
and has spent much time with poetry, knows well
that Zeus once loved the lovely Semele;
he knows that Dawn, the bright light of the world,
once ravished Cephalus hence to the gods' company   455
for love's sake. Yet they still dwell in heaven
and do not flee in exile from the gods—
they are content, I am sure, to be subdued
by the stroke of love.
But you, you won't submit? Why, you should certainly
have had your father beget you on fixed terms   460
or with other gods for masters, if you don't like
the laws that rule this world. Tell me, how many
men of good enough sense do you suppose
turn a blind eye to the sickness of their marriage;
how many fathers have helped their erring sons
procure a lover? It is the wise man's part   465
to leave in darkness everything that is ugly.

    We should not in the conduct of our lives
be too exacting. Look, see this roof here—
these overarching beams that span your house—
could builders with all their skill lay them dead straight?
You've fallen into the great sea of love
and with your puny swimming would escape!   470
If in the sum you have more good than bad,
count yourself fortunate—for you are mortal.

    Come on, dear child, give up your wicked thoughts.
Give up your insolence. It's only insolent pride

to wish to be superior to the gods.   475
Endure your love. A god has willed it so.
Indeed, you are sick. So try to find some means
to turn your sickness into health again.
There are magic love charms, spells of enchantment;
we'll find some remedy for your lovesickness.
Men would take long to hunt devices out,   480
if we the women did not find them first.

CHORUS LEADER
Phaedra, indeed she speaks more usefully
for this present trouble. But it is you I praise.
And yet my praise brings with it more discomfort
than do her words: it is bitterer to the ear.   485

PHAEDRA
This is the deadly thing that devastates
well-ordered cities and the homes of men—
this art of all-too-attractive-sounding words.
It's not the words ringing delight in the ear
that one should speak, but those that have the power
to save their hearer's honorable name.

NURSE
This is high moralizing! What you need   490
is not fine words, but the man! Come, let's be done,
and tell your story frankly and directly.
For if there were not such danger to your life,
or if you were a pure and temperate woman,
I never would have led you on so far,   495
merely to please your fancy or your lust.
But now a great prize hangs on our endeavors,
and that's the saving of a life—yours, Phaedra!
There's none can blame us for our actions now.

PHAEDRA
What you say is wicked, wicked! Hold your tongue!
I will not hear such shameful words again.

NURSE

    Oh, they are shameful! But for you they're better   500
    than noble-sounding moral sentiments.
    The deed is better if it saves your life
    than your good name in which you die exulting.

PHAEDRA

    For the gods' sake, do not proceed any further!
    What you say sounds good, but is terrible!
    My very soul is subdued by my love
    and if you plead the cause of wrong so well   505
    I'll fall into the ruin that now I flee.

NURSE

    If that is what you think, ideally, you'd be virtuous;
    But if not, you should obey me: that's next best.
    It has just come to my mind, I have in the house   510
    some magic love charms. They will end your trouble;
    they'll neither harm your honor nor your mind.
    They'll end your trouble . . . only you must be brave.
    But first we need from him you desire some token—
    a lock of his hair or some piece of his clothes—
    we'll take this and make one joy out of two.   515

PHAEDRA

    This charm: is it an ointment or a drink?

NURSE

    I don't know. Don't be overanxious, child,
    to find out what it is. Accept its benefits.

PHAEDRA

    I fear you will be too clever for my good.

NURSE

    You are afraid of everything. What is it you fear?

PHAEDRA

    You surely will not tell this to Theseus' son?   520

NURSE

Come, let that be: I will arrange all well.
Only, my lady Cypris of the Sea,
be my helper you. The other thoughts I have
I'll tell to those we love within the house;
that will suffice.

(*Exit the Nurse into the house.*)

CHORUS [*singing*]

STROPHE A

Eros, Eros that distills desire upon the eyes,   525
that brings bewitching grace into the heart
of those you would destroy:
I pray that you may never come to me
with murderous intent,
in rhythms measureless and wild.
Not fire nor stars have stronger bolts   530
than those of Aphrodite sent
by the hand of Eros, Zeus's child.

ANTISTROPHE A

In vain, in vain by Alpheus' stream,   535
in the halls of Phoebus' Pythian shrine
the land of Greece increases sacrifice.
But Eros the king of men we honor not,   540
although he keeps the keys
of the temple of desire,
although he goes destroying through the world,
author of dread calamities
and ruin when he enters human hearts.

STROPHE B

The untamed Oechalian filly who had never known   545
the bed of love, known neither man nor marriage,
the goddess Cypris gave her to Heracles.
She took her from the home of Eurytus,

maiden unhappy in her marriage song,
wild as a Naiad or a Bacchant, 550
with blood and fire, a murderous wedding song!

ANTISTROPHE B

O holy walls of Thebes and Dirce's fountain 555
bear witness you, to Cypris' grim journeying:
once you saw her bring Semele to bed,
lull her to sleep, clasped in the arms of Death,
pregnant with Dionysus by the thunder king. 560
Love is like a flitting bee in the world's garden,
and for its flowers destruction is in its breath.

PHAEDRA   (Listening at the door.)
Women, be silent!
Oh, I am destroyed forever. 565

CHORUS LEADER
What is there terrible within the house?

PHAEDRA
Hush, let me hear the voices within!

CHORUS LEADER
And I obey. But this is sorrow's prelude.

PHAEDRA
Oh no!
Oh, I am the most miserable of women! 570

CHORUS [singing, while Phaedra speaks]
What does she mean by her cries?
Why does she scream?
Tell us the fear-winged word, mistress,
rushing upon the heart.

PHAEDRA
I am lost. Go, women, stand and listen there yourselves 575
and hear the tumult that falls on the house.

CHORUS

Mistress, you stand at the door.
It is you who can tell us best
what happens within the house.
Tell me, tell me, what evil has befallen.   580

PHAEDRA

It is the son of the horse-loving Amazon,
Hippolytus, cursing my servant maid.

CHORUS

My ears can catch a sound,   585
but I can hear nothing clear.
I can only hear a voice that has come,
that has come through the door.

PHAEDRA

It is plain enough. He cries aloud against
the mischievous bawd who betrays her master's bed.   590

CHORUS

Lady, you are betrayed!
How can I help you?
What was hidden is revealed.
You are destroyed.
Those you love have betrayed you.   595

PHAEDRA

She loved me and she told him of my troubles,
and so has ruined me. She was my doctor,
but her cure has made my illness fatal now.

CHORUS LEADER

What will you do? There is no cure any more.

PHAEDRA

I know of one, and only one—quick death.
That is the only cure for my disease.   600

(Enter Hippolytus and the Nurse from the house.)°

HIPPOLYTUS

O Mother Earth! O Sun and open sky!
What words I have heard from this accursed tongue!

NURSE

Hush, son! Someone may hear you shouting.

HIPPOLYTUS

You cannot expect that I'll hear horror in silence!

NURSE

I beg you, by your strong right hand, don't speak!   605

HIPPOLYTUS

Don't lay your hand on me! Let go my cloak!

NURSE

By your knees then . . . don't destroy me!

HIPPOLYTUS

                                    What is this?
Don't you declare that you have done nothing wrong?

NURSE

Yes, but the story, son, is not for everyone.

HIPPOLYTUS

Why not? A pleasant tale makes pleasanter telling,
when there are many listeners.   610

NURSE

You will not break your oath to me, surely you will not?

HIPPOLYTUS

My tongue swore, but my mind was quite unpledged.

NURSE

Son, what would you do? You'll not destroy your friends?

HIPPOLYTUS

"Friends"!
I spit the word away. None of the wicked
are friends of mine.

NURSE

                              Then pardon, son. It's natural
that we should make mistakes, since we are human.   615

HIPPOLYTUS

Women! This coin which men find counterfeit!
Why, why, Lord Zeus, did you put them in the world,
in the light of the sun? If you were so determined
to breed the race of man, the source of it
should not have been women. Men might have dedicated
in your own temples images of gold,   620
iron, or weight of bronze, and thus have bought
the seed of progeny . . . to each been given
his worth in sons according to the assessment
of his gift's value. So we might have lived
in houses free of the taint of women's presence.
But now, to bring this plague into our houses   625
we destroy° the fortunes of our homes. In this
we have a proof how great a curse is woman.
For the father who begets her, rears her up,
must add a dowry gift to pack her off
to another's house and thus be rid of the load.
And he again that takes the cursed creature   630
rejoices and enriches his heart's jewel
with dear adornment, beauty heaped on vileness.
With lovely clothes the poor wretch tricks her out
spending the wealth that underprops his house.
For of necessity either one weds well,°
rejoicing in his in-laws, but must keep   635
a bitter bed; or else his marriage works
but his in-laws are useless, so that benefit
is all he has to counteract misfortune.

That husband has the easiest life whose wife
is a mere nothingness, a simple fool,
uselessly sitting by the fireside.   640
I hate a clever woman—yes, I pray
that I may never have a wife at home
with more than woman's wits! Lust breeds mischief
in the clever ones. The limits of their minds
deny the stupid ones lecherous delights.
We should not suffer servants to approach them,   645
but give them as companions voiceless beasts,
dumb—but with teeth, that they might not converse,
and hear another voice in answer.
But now at home the mistress plots the mischief,
and the maid carries it abroad.

                    So you, vile woman,   650
came here to me to bargain and to traffic
in the sanctity of my father's marriage bed.
I'll go to a running stream and pour its waters
into my ear to purge away the filth.
Shall I who cannot even hear such impurity,
and feel myself untouched—shall I turn wicked?   655
Woman, know this. It is my piety saves you.
Had you not caught me off guard and bound
my lips with an oath, by heaven I would not refrain
from telling this to my father.
Now I will go and leave this house until
Theseus returns from his foreign wanderings,
and I'll be silent. But I'll watch you close.   660
I'll walk with my father step by step and see
how you look at him . . . you and your mistress both.
I have tasted of the daring of your infamy.
I'll know it for the future.° Curses on you!
I'll hate you women, hate and hate and hate you,
and never have enough of hating . . .

                         Some
say that I talk of this eternally,   665

yes, but eternal, too, is woman's wickedness.
Either let someone teach them to be temperate,
or allow me to trample on them forever.

(Exit Hippolytus to the side.)

PHAEDRA° [singing]

ANTISTROPHE

Bitter indeed is woman's destiny!
I have failed. What trick is there now, what cunning plea   670
to loose the knot around my neck?
I have had justice. Oh, earth and the sunlight!
Where shall I escape from my fate?
How shall I hide my trouble, dear friends?
What God or man would appear
to bear hand or part in my crime?   675
There is a limit to all suffering and I have reached it.
I am the unhappiest of women.

NURSE°

Alas, mistress, all is over now.   680
your servant's schemes have failed and you are ruined.

PHAEDRA

This is fine service you have rendered me,
corrupted, damned seducer of your friends!
May Zeus, the father of my father's line,
blot you out utterly, raze you from the world
with thunderbolts! Did I not see your purpose,   685
did I not say to you, "Breathe not a word of this"
which now overwhelms me with shame? But you,
you did not hold back. And so it's without honor
that I will die.
Enough of this. We need a new scheme now.
The anger of Hippolytus is whetted.
He will tell his father all the wrongs you did,   690
to my disparagement. He will tell old Pittheus, too.
He will fill all the land with my dishonor.

May my curse
light upon you, on you and all the others
who eagerly help unwilling friends to ruin.

NURSE

Mistress, you may well blame my ill success,   695
for sorrow's bite is master of your judgment.
But I have an answer to make if you will listen.
I reared you up. I am your loyal servant.
I sought a remedy for your love's sickness,
and found . . . not what I sought.
Had I succeeded, I'd have been a wise one.   700
Our wisdom varies in proportion to
our failure or achievement.

PHAEDRA

                          So, that's enough
for me? Do I have justice if you deal me
my deathblow and then say "I was wrong: I grant it"?

NURSE

We talk too long. True, I was not wise then.
But even from this desperate plight, my child,   705
you can escape.

PHAEDRA

                          You, speak no more to me.
You gave me then dishonorable advice.
And what you tried has brought dishonor too.
Away with you!
Think of yourself. For me and my concerns
I will arrange all well.

                    (Exit Nurse into the house.)

You noble ladies of Troezen, grant me this,   710
this one request, that what you have heard here
you wrap in silence.

CHORUS LEADER

    I swear by holy Artemis, child of Zeus,
    never to bring your troubles to the daylight.

PHAEDRA

    I thank you. I have found one sole device   715
    in this unhappy business, one alone,
    so that I can pass on to my children after me
    life with an uncontaminated name,
    and myself profit by the present throw
    of Fortune's dice. For I will never shame you,
    my Cretan home, nor will I go to face   720
    Theseus, defendant on an ugly charge,
    never—for one life's sake.

CHORUS LEADER

    What is the desperate deed you mean to do,
    the deed past cure?

PHAEDRA

                       To die. But the way of it, that
    is what I now must plan.

CHORUS LEADER

                  Oh, do not speak of it!

PHAEDRA

    No, I'll not speak of it. But on this day
    when I shake off the burden of this life   725
    I shall delight the goddess who destroys me,
    the goddess Cypris.
    Bitter will have been the love that conquers me,
    but in my death I shall at least bring sorrow
    upon another, too, that his high heart
    may know no arrogant joy at my life's shipwreck;
    he will have his share in this my mortal sickness   730
    and learn to be more temperate himself.

(Exit Phaedra into the house.)

CHORUS [*singing*]

STROPHE A

Would that I were under the cliffs, in the secret hiding places of
    the rocks,
that a god might change me to a wingèd bird
and set me among the feathered flocks.
I would rise and fly to where the sea   735
washes the Adriatic coast,
and to the waters of Eridanus.
Into that deep-blue tide,
where their father, the Sun, goes down,
the unhappy maidens weep
tears from their amber-gleaming eyes   740
in pity for Phaethon.

ANTISTROPHE A

I would win my way to the coast,
apple-bearing Hesperian coast,
of which the minstrels sing,
where the lord of the ocean
denies the voyager further sailing,   745
and fixes the solemn limit of heaven
which giant Atlas upholds.
There the streams flow with ambrosia
by Zeus's bed of love,
and holy Earth the giver of life,   750
yields to the gods rich blessedness.

STROPHE B

O Cretan ship with the white sails,
from a happy home you brought her,
my mistress over the tossing foam, over the salty sea   755
to bless her with a marriage unblessed.
Black was the omen that sped her here,

black was the omen for both her lands,
for glorious Athens and her Cretan home,
as they bound to Munychia's beach   760
the cables' ends with their twisted strands
and stepped ashore on the continent.

ANTISTROPHE B

The presage of the omen was true;   765
Aphrodite has broken her spirit
with the terrible sickness of impious love.
The waves of destruction are over her head,
from the roof of her room with its marriage bed,
she will tie the twisted noose.   770
And it will go around her fair white neck!
She felt shame at her cruel fate.
She has chosen good name rather than life:
she is easing her heart of its bitter load of love.   775

NURSE   (Within.)

Ho, there, help!
You who are near the palace, help!
My mistress, Theseus' wife, has hanged herself.

CHORUS LEADER

It is done, she is hanged in the dangling rope.
Our queen is dead.

NURSE   (Within.)

Quick! Someone bring a knife!   780
Help me cut the knot around her neck.

(Individual members of the Chorus speak.)

FIRST WOMAN

What shall we do, friends? Shall we cross the threshold,
and take the queen from the grip of the tight-drawn cords?

SECOND WOMAN

Why should we? There are servants enough within

for that. Where outsiders intervene,
there is no safety.   785

NURSE   (*Within.*)

Lay her out straight, poor lady.
Bitter shall my lord find this housekeeping.

THIRD WOMAN

From what I hear, the queen is dead.
They are already laying out the corpse.

(*Theseus enters from the side.*)

THESEUS

Women, what is this crying in the house?   790
I heard heavy wailing on the wind,
as it were servants, mourning. And my house
deigns me, a returning envoy, no warm welcome.
The doors are shut against me. Can it be
something has happened to my father? He is old.   795
His life has traveled a great journey,
but bitter would be his passing from our house.

CHORUS LEADER

Theseus, it's not the old that trouble has struck.
Young is the dead one, and bitterly you'll grieve.

THESEUS

My children . . . has death snatched a life away?

CHORUS LEADER

Your children live—but sorrowfully, King.   800
Their mother is dead.

THESEUS

                              It cannot be true, it cannot.
My wife! How could she be dead?

CHORUS LEADER

She herself tied a rope around her neck.

THESEUS

Was it grief and numbing loneliness drove her to it,
or has some misadventure been at work?

CHORUS LEADER

I know no more than this. I, too, came lately
to mourn for you and yours, King Theseus.   805

THESEUS

Oh,
why did I plait this coronal of leaves,
and crown my head with garlands, I the envoy
who find my journey end in misery?
Servants! Open the doors! Unbar the fastenings,
that I may see this bitter sight, my wife
who killed me in her own death.   810

                    (The door is opened, revealing Phaedra's corpse.)

CHORUS [in the following exchange, the Chorus sings, the Chorus Leader
speaks, and Theseus sings the lines in italics and speaks the others]

Woman unhappy, tortured,
your suffering, your death,
has shaken this house to its foundations.
You were daring, you who died
in violence and guilt.
Here was a wrestling: your own hand against your life.   815
Who can have cast a shadow on your life?

THESEUS

                              STROPHE

Bitterness of sorrow!
Extremest sorrow that a man can suffer!
Fate, you have ground me and my house to dust,
fate in the form of some ineffable
pollution, some grim spirit of revenge.   820
The file has whittled away my life until
it is a life no more.

I am like a swimmer that falls into a great sea:
I cannot cross this towering wave I see before me.   825
My wife! I cannot think
of anything said or done to drive you to this horrible death.
You are like a bird that has vanished out of my hand.
You have made a quick leap out of my arms
into the land of Death.
It must be the sin of one of my ancestors in the dim past   830
gods in their vengeance make me pay now.

CHORUS LEADER

You are not the only one, King.
Many another as well as you
has lost a noble wife.   835

THESEUS

ANTISTROPHE

Darkness beneath the earth, darkness beneath the earth!
How good to lie there and be dead,
now that I have lost you, my dearest companion.
Your death is no less mine.   840
Where did this deadly misfortune come from,
poor woman, upon your heart?
Will any of you
tell me what happened?
Or does the palace keep a flock of you for nothing?
Oh,° the pain I saw in the house!
I cannot speak of it, I cannot bear it. I am a dead man.   845
My house is empty and my children orphaned.
You have left them, left them, you
my darling wife—
the best of wives   850
of all the sun looks down on or the blazing stars of the night.

CHORUS

Woe for the house! Such storms of ill assail it.
My eyes are wells of tears and overrun,
and still I fear the evil that shall come.   855

THESEUS

But wait a moment!
What is this tablet fastened to her dear hand?
Does it want to tell me some news?
Has the poor woman written begging me to care
for our marriage and children?
Sad one, rest confident.   860
There is no woman in the world who shall come to this house
and sleep by my side.
Look, the familiar golden signet ring,
hers who was once my wife, beckons me!
Come, I will break the seals,
and see what this letter wants to tell me.   865

CHORUS

Surely some god
brings sorrow upon sorrow in succession.°
The house of our lords is destroyed: it is no more.   870

CHORUS LEADER

God, if it so may be, hear my prayer.°
Do not destroy this house utterly. I am a prophet:
I can see the omen of coming trouble.

THESEUS

Alas, here is endless sorrow upon sorrow.
It passes speech, passes endurance.   875

CHORUS LEADER

What is it? Tell us if we may share the story.

THESEUS

It cries aloud, this tablet, cries aloud,
and Death is its song!
How shall I escape this weight of evils? I am ruined, destroyed.
What a song I have seen, sung in this writing!   880

CHORUS LEADER

Ah! Your speech shows a prelude of ruin!

THESEUS

I shall no longer hold this secret prisoner
in the gates of my mouth. It is horrible,
yet I will speak.
Citizens!
Hippolytus has dared to rape my wife.   885
He has dishonored Zeus's holy sunlight.
Father Poseidon, once you gave to me
three curses. . . . Now with one of these, I pray,
kill my son. Suffer him not to escape
this very day, if you have promised truly.   890

CHORUS LEADER

Call back your curses, King, call back your curses.
Else you will realize that you were wrong
another day, too late. I pray you, trust me.

THESEUS

I will not. And I now make this addition:
I banish him from this land's boundaries.
So fate shall strike him, one way or the other,
either Poseidon will respect my curse,   895
and send him dead into the house of Hades,
or exiled from this land, a beggar wandering,
on foreign soil, his life shall suck the dregs
of sorrow's cup.

CHORUS LEADER

Here comes your son, at the right moment, King Theseus.
Give over your deadly anger, you will best   900
determine for the welfare of your house.

(Enter Hippolytus with cosmpanions from the side.)

HIPPOLYTUS

I heard you crying, father, and came quickly.
I know no cause why you should mourn.
Tell me.

(He sees the body of Phaedra.)

O father, father—I see your wife! She's dead!   905
I cannot believe it. But a few moments since
I left her. . . . And just now she was still alive.
But what could it be? How did she die, father?
I must hear the truth from you. You say nothing to me?   910
When you are in trouble is no time for silence.
The heart that would hear everything
is proved most greedy in misfortune's hour.
You should not hide your troubles from your friends,
and, father, those who are closer than your friends.   915

THESEUS

What fools men are! You work and work for nothing,
you teach ten thousand skills to one another,
invent, discover everything. One thing only
you do not know: one thing you never hunted for—
a way to teach intelligence to fools.   920

HIPPOLYTUS

Clever indeed
would be the teacher able to compel
the stupid to be wise! But this is no time
for such fine logic chopping.
              I am afraid
your tongue runs wild through sorrow.

THESEUS

              If there were
some token now, some mark to make the division   925
clear between friend and friend, the true and the false!
All men should have two voices, one the just voice,
and one as chance would have it. In this way
the treacherous scheming voice would be confuted   930
by the just, and we should never be deceived.

HIPPOLYTUS

Has some friend poisoned your ear and slandered me?
Am I suspected despite my innocence?
I am amazed. I am amazed to hear
your words. They are distraught. They go indeed
far wide of the mark!   935

THESEUS

The mind of man—how far will it advance?
Where will its daring impudence find limits?
If human villainy and human life
shall grow in due proportion during a man's life,
if the one who's later shall always grow in wickedness
past the earlier, the gods must add another   940
world to this one, to hold all the villains.
   Look at this man! He is my son and he
dishonored my wife's bed! By the dead's testimony
he's clearly proved the vilest, falsest wretch.   945
Come—since you have already reached depravity—
show me your face; show it to me, your father.
   So you are the veritable holy man?
You walked with gods in purity immaculate?
I'll not believe your arrogant boasts: the gods   950
are not at all so stupid as you think.
Go, boast that you eat no meat, that you have Orpheus
for your king. Read until you are demented
your great thick books whose substance is as smoke.
For I have found you out. I tell you all,   955
avoid such men as he. They hunt their prey
with holy-seeming words, but their designs
are black and ugly. She is dead. You thought
that this would save you? Wretch, it is chiefly that
which proves your guilt. What oath that you can swear,   960
what speech that you can make for your acquittal,
outweighs her body here? You'll say, to be sure,

she was your enemy and that the bastard son
is always hateful to the legitimate line.
Your words would argue her a foolish merchant
whose stock of merchandise was her own life,
if she should throw away what she held dearest
to gratify her enmity for you.   965

    Or will you tell me that this frantic folly
is part of woman's nature but a man
is different? Yet I know that young men
are no more to be trusted than are women
when Cypris disturbs the youthful blood in them.
But the very male in them helps and protects them.   970
But why should I debate against you in words?
Here is the woman dead, the surest witness.
Get from this land with all the speed you can
to exile—may you rot there! Never again
come to our city, god-built Athens, nor
to any land over which my spear is king.   975

    If I should take this injury at your hands
and pardon you, then Sinis of the Isthmus,
whom once I killed, would vow I never killed him,
but only bragged of the deed. And Sciron's rocks
washed by the sea would call me liar when
I swore I was a terror to ill-doers.   980

CHORUS LEADER
    I cannot say of any man: he is happy.
See here how former happiness lies uprooted!

HIPPOLYTUS
    Your furious spirit is terrifying, father:
but this subject, though it's dressed in eloquence,
if you will lay the matter bare of words,   985
you'll find it is not eloquent. I am
no man to speak with vapid, precious skill
before a mob, although among my equals

and in a narrow circle I am held
not unaccomplished as a speaker.
That is as it should be. The demagogue
who charms a crowd is scorned by wiser judges.
But here in this necessity I must speak.   990
First I shall take the argument you first
urged as so irrefutable and deadly.
You see the earth and air about you, father?
In all of that there lives no man more pure
or temperate than I, though you deny it.   995
      It is my rule to honor the gods first
and then to have as friends only such men
as try to do no wrong, men who feel shame
at ordering evil or treating others meanly
in return for kindness. I am no mocker
of my companions. Those who are my friends   1000
find me as much their friend when they are absent
as when we are together.
      There is one thing that I have never done, the thing
of which you think that you convict me, father.
I am a virgin to this very day.
Save what I have heard or what I have seen in pictures,   1005
I'm ignorant of the deed. Nor do I wish
to see such things, for I've a maiden soul.
But say you disbelieve my temperance.
Then tell me how I came to be corrupted:
was it because she was more beautiful
than all the other women in the world?   1010
Or did I think that by taking her,
I'd win your place and kingdom for a dowry
and live in your own house? I would have been
a fool, a senseless fool, if I had dreamed it.
Was monarchy so sweet? Never, I tell you,
for the wise. A man whom power has so enchanted
must be demented. I would wish to be   1015

first in the athletic contests of the Greeks,
but in the city I'd take second place
and an enduring happy life among
the best society who are my friends.
So one can do what he wants, and danger's absence
has charms above the royal diadem.   1020

    But one word more and my defense is finished.
If I possessed a witness to my character,
if I were tried when she still saw the light,
deeds would have helped you as you scanned your friends
to know the true from the false. But now I swear,
I swear to you by Zeus, the god of oaths,   1025
by this deep-rooted fundament of earth,
I never did you wrong with your own wife
nor would have wished or even thought of it.
If I have been a villain, may I die
unfamed, unknown, a homeless stateless beggar,
an exile! May the earth and sea refuse   1030
to take my body in when I am dead!

    Out of what fear your wife took her own life
I do not know. More I may not say.
Pure she was in deed, although not pure:
I that have purity have used it to my ruin.   1035

CHORUS LEADER
    You have rebutted the charge enough by your oath:
    it is a great pledge you took in the gods' name.

THESEUS
    Why, here's a spell-binding magician for you!
    He wrongs his father and then trusts his craft,
    his smooth beguiling craft to lull my anger.   1040

HIPPOLYTUS
    Father, I must wonder at this in you.
    If I were your father now, and you my son,

I would not have banished you to exile! I
would have killed you if I thought you touched my wife.

THESEUS

This speech is worthy of you: but you'll not die so,   1045
by this rule that you have laid down for yourself.
A quick death is the easiest of ends
for a miserable man. No, you'll go wandering
far from your fatherland and beg your way
in foreign lands, draining dry a bitter life.
This is the payment of the impious man.°   1050

HIPPOLYTUS

What will you do? You will not wait until
time's pointing finger proves me innocent?
Must I then go at once to banishment?

THESEUS

Yes, and had I the power, your place of exile
would be beyond Pontus and Atlas' pillars.
That is the measure of my hate, my son.

HIPPOLYTUS

Pledges, oaths, and oracles—you will not test them?   1055
You will banish me from the kingdom without trial?

THESEUS

This letter here is proof without lot-casting.
As for the birds that fly above my head:
a long good-bye to them.

HIPPOLYTUS

                              Eternal gods!
Why don't I speak, since I am ruined now   1060
through loyalty to the oath I took by you?
No, he would not believe who should believe,
and I should be false to my oath for nothing.

THESEUS

Here's more of that holy and haughty manner of yours!
I cannot stomach it. Away with you!
Get from this country—and go quickly!   1065

HIPPOLYTUS

Where shall I turn? What friend will take me in,
when I am banished on a charge like this?

THESEUS

Doubtless some man who loves to entertain
a wife's seducer, a housemate in wickedness.

HIPPOLYTUS

That blow went home.   1070
I am near crying when I think that I
am judged to be wicked and that it is you who are judge.

THESEUS

You should have sobbed and thought of that before,
when you resolved to rape your father's wife.

HIPPOLYTUS

My house, if only you could speak for me!
Take voice and testify if I am wicked.   1075

THESEUS

You have a clever trick of citing witnesses
whose testimony is mute. Here is your handiwork.

(He points to the body.)

It, too, can't speak—but it convicts you.

HIPPOLYTUS

Ah!
If I could only find
another me to look me in the face
and see my tears and all that I am suffering!

THESEUS

    Yes, in self-worship you are certainly practiced.   1080
    You are more at home there than in the other virtues,
    justice, for instance, and duty toward a father.

HIPPOLYTUS

    Unhappy mother mine, and bitter birth pangs,
    when you gave me to the world! I would not wish
    on any of my friends a bastard's birth.

THESEUS   *(To the servants.)*

    Drag him away!
    Did you not hear me, men, a long time since
    proclaiming his decree of banishment?   1085

HIPPOLYTUS

    Let one of them touch me at his peril! But you,
    you drive me out yourself—if you have the heart!

THESEUS

    I'll do it, too, unless you obey my orders.
    No pity for your exile will change my heart.

                              (Exit Theseus into the house.)

HIPPOLYTUS

    So, I'm condemned and there is no escape.   1090
    I know the truth but cannot tell the truth.

                         (To the statue of Artemis.)

    Daughter of Leto, dearest of the gods to me,
    comrade and partner in the hunt, behold me,
    banished from famous Athens.
    Farewell, city! Farewell, Erechtheus' land!   1095
    Troezen, farewell! So many happy times
    you knew to give a young man, growing up.
    This is the last time I shall look upon you,
    the last time I shall greet you.

(To his companions.)

Come friends, you are of my age and of this country,
say your farewells and set me on my way.
You'll never see a man more pure and temperate—   1100
even if my father thinks that I am not.

(Exit Hippolytus to the side.)

CHORUS OF HUNTSMEN° [*singing*]
                    STROPHE A
The care of the gods for us is a great thing,
whenever it comes to my mind:
it plucks the burden of sorrow from me.
So I have a secret hope of knowledge;   1105
but my hopes grow dim when I see
the deeds of men and their destinies.
For fortune is ever veering, and the currents of men's lives are
*   shifting,*
wandering forever.   1110

CHORUS OF WOMEN [*singing*]
                    ANTISTROPHE A
This is the lot in life I seek
and I pray that the gods may grant it me,
luck and prosperity
and a heart untroubled by anguish;
and a mind that is neither inflexible
nor false clipped coin,   1115
that I may easily change my ways,
my ways of today when tomorrow comes,
and so be happy all my life long.

CHORUS OF HUNTSMEN°
                    STROPHE B
My heart is no longer clear: 1120
I have seen what I never dreamed.

I have seen the brightest star of Athens,°
stricken by a father's wrath,
banished to an alien land. 1125
Sands of the seashore!
Thicket of the mountain!
Where with his pacing hounds
he hunted wild beasts and killed
to the honor of holy Dictynna. 1130

CHORUS OF WOMEN

ANTISTROPHE B

He will never again mount his car
with its span of Venetian mares,
nor fill the ring of Limnae with the sound of horses' hoofs.
The music that never slept
on the strings of his lyre, shall be mute, 1135
shall be mute in his father's house.
The haunts of the maiden goddess
in the deep, rich meadow shall lack their crowns.
You are banished: there's an end 1140
of the rivalry of maids for your love.

EPODE

But my sorrow shall not die;
still my eyes shall be wet with tears
for your dreadful doom.
Sad mother, you bore him in vain; 1145
I am angry against the gods.
Sister Graces, why did you let him go,
guiltless, out of his native land,
out of his father's house? 1150

CHORUS LEADER

But here I see Hippolytus' servant,
in haste making for the house, his face sorrowful.

(Enter a Messenger° from the side.)

MESSENGER

Where shall I go to find King Theseus, women?
If you know, tell me. Is he within doors?   1155

CHORUS

Here he is coming out.

MESSENGER

Theseus, I bring you news worthy of distress
for you and all the citizens who live
in Athens' walls and boundaries of Troezen.

THESEUS

What is it? Has some still newer disaster   1160
seized my two neighboring cities?

MESSENGER

Hippolytus is dead: I may almost say dead:
he sees the light of day still, though the balance
that holds him in this world is slight indeed.

THESEUS

Who killed him? I can guess that someone hated him,
whose wife he raped, as he did mine, his father's.   1165

MESSENGER

It was the horses of his own car that killed him,
they, and the curses of your lips,
the curses you invoked against your son,
and prayed the lord of ocean to fulfill them.

THESEUS

O gods—Poseidon, you are then truly
my father! You have heard my prayers!   1170
How did he die? Tell me. How did the beam
of Justice's deadfall strike him, my dishonorer?

MESSENGER

We were combing our horses' coats beside the sea,

where the waves came crashing to the shore. And we were
    crying,
for one had come and told us that our master,   1175
Hippolytus, should walk this land no more,
since you had laid hard banishment upon him.
Then he came himself down to the shore to us,
with the same refrain of tears,
and with him walked a countless company
of friends and young men his own age.   1180
    But at last he gave over crying and said:
"Why do I rave like this? It is my father
who has commanded and I must obey him.
Prepare my horses, men, and harness them.
For this no longer is a city of mine."
Then every man made haste. Before you could say the words,   1185
we had made the horses ready before our master.
He put his feet into the driver's rings,
and took the reins from the rail into his hands.
But first he folded his hands and prayed the gods: 1190
"Zeus, let me die now, if I have been wicked!
Let my father perceive that he has done me wrong,
whether I live to see the day or not."
    With that, he took the goad and touched the horses.
And we his servants followed our master's car,   1195
close by the horses' heads, on the straight road
that leads to Argos and to Epidaurus.
When we were entering the lonely country
the other side of the border, where the shore   1200
goes down to the Saronic Gulf, a rumbling
deep down in the earth, terrible to hear,
roared loudly like the thunder of Father Zeus.
The horses raised their heads, pricked up their ears,
and mighty fear was on us all to know
whence came the sound. As we looked toward the shore,   1205
where the waves were beating, we saw a wave appear,

a miracle wave, lifting its crest to the sky,
so high that Sciron's coast was blotted out
from my eye's vision. And it hid the Isthmus
and the Asclepius Rock. To the shore it came, 1210
swelling, boiling, crashing, casting its surf around,
to where the chariot stood.
But at the very moment when it broke,
the wave threw up a monstrous savage bull.
Its bellowing filled the land, and the land echoed it, 1215
with shuddering emphasis. And for those who saw it
the sight was too great to bear. Then sudden panic
fell on the horses in the car. But the master—
he was used to horses' ways—all his life long
he had been with horses—took firm grip of the reins 1220
and lashed the ends behind his back and pulled
like a sailor at the oar. The horses bolted:
their teeth were clenched upon the fire-forged bit.
They heeded neither the driver's hand nor harness
nor the jointed car. As often as he would turn them 1225
with guiding hand to the soft sand of the shore,
the bull appeared in front to head them off,
maddening the team with terror.
But when in frenzy they charged toward the cliffs, 1230
the bull came galloping beside the rail,
silently following—until he brought disaster,
capsizing the car, striking the wheel on a rock.
Then all was in confusion. The naves of wheels
and axle pins flew up into the air, 1235
and he the unlucky driver, tangled in the reins,
was dragged along in an inextricable
knot, and his dear head pounded on the rocks,
his body bruised. He cried aloud and terrible
his voice rang in our ears: "Stand, horses, stand! 1240
You were fed in my stables. Do not kill me!
My father's curse! His curse! Will none of you
save me? I am a good, true man. Save me!"

Many of us had will enough, but all
were left behind. Cut somehow free of the reins,
he fell. There was still a little life in him.   1245
But the horses vanished and that ill-omened monster,
somewhere, I know not where, in the rough cliffs.
    I am only a slave in your household, your majesty,
but I shall never be able to believe   1250
that your son was wicked, not though the race of women
were all hanged for it, not though they filled with writing
the whole of the pine forest on Mount Ida—
for I know that he's a good and noble man.

CHORUS LEADER
    It has been fulfilled, this bitter, new disaster: 1255
    from what is doomed and fated there's no escape.

THESEUS
    For hatred of the sufferer I was glad
    at what you told me. Still, he was my son.
    As such I have reverence for him and for the gods:
    I neither rejoice nor sorrow at these evils.   1260

MESSENGER
    What is your pleasure that we do with him?
    Would you have him brought to you? If I might counsel,
    do not be harsh with your son—now that he's ruined.

THESEUS
    Bring him to me that I may see his face.   1265
    He swore that he had never wronged my bed.
    I'll refute him with the gods' own punishing stroke.

                              (*Exit Messenger to the side.*)

CHORUS [*singing*]
    Cypris, you guide the inflexible hearts of gods
    and of men,
    and with you
    comes Eros with the flashing wings,   1270

with the swiftest of wings.
Over the earth he flies
and the loud-echoing salt sea.
Winged, golden, he bewitches and maddens the heart
of the victim he swoops upon.   1275
He bewitches the whelps of the mountains
and of the sea,
and all the creatures that earth feeds,
and the blazing sun sees—
and men, too—
over all you hold royal dominion,   1280
Cypris, you are only ruler
over all these.

(Artemis appears on the roof of the house.)

ARTEMIS [chanting]
I call on you, noble son of Aegeus,
to hear me! It is I,
Artemis, child of Leto.   1285
   Theseus, poor man, what joy have you here?
You have murdered your son most impiously.
Dark indeed was the conclusion
you drew from your wife's lying stories,
but plain to see is the destruction
to which they led you.
There's a hell underground: haste to it,   1290
and hide your head there! Or will you take wings,
choose the life of a bird instead of a man,
keep your feet from treading destruction's path?
Among good men, at least, you have no share in life.   1295

[speaking]

   Hear, Theseus, how these evils came to pass.
I shall gain nothing, but I'll give you pain.
I've come for this—to show that your son's heart
was always just, so that in his death

his good name may live on. I will show you, too,
the frenzied love that seized your wife, or I may call it   1300
a noble innocence. For that most hated goddess,
hated by all of us whose joy is virginity,
drove her with love's sharp prickings to desire
your son. She tried her best to vanquish Cypris
with the mind's power, but at last against her will
she was destroyed by the nurse's stratagems,   1305
who told your son under oath her mistress loved him.
But he, just man, did not fall in with her
counsels, and even when reviled by you
refused to break the oath that he had pledged.
Such was his piety. But your wife feared
lest she be put to the proof and wrote a letter,   1310
a letter full of lies; and so she killed
your son by treachery; but she convinced you.

THESEUS
   Alas!

ARTEMIS
   This is a bitter story, Theseus. Stay,
   hear further, that you may sorrow all the more.
   You know you had three curses from your father,   1315
   three, clear for you to use? One you have launched,
   vile wretch, at your own son, when you might have
   spent it upon an enemy. Your father,
   king of the sea, in loving kindness to you
   gave you, as he had promised, all he ought.
   But you've been proven wicked both in his eyes   1320
   and mine in that you did not stay for oaths
   nor voice of oracles, nor put to proof,
   nor let long time investigate—too quickly
   you hurled the curses at your son and killed him.

THESEUS
   Mistress, I am destroyed.

ARTEMIS

What you have done indeed is dreadful—but   1325
you still might gain forgiveness for these things.
For it was Cypris managed the thing this way
to gratify her anger against Hippolytus.
This is the settled custom of the gods:
No one may fly in the face of another's wish:
we remain aloof and neutral. Else, I assure you,   1330
had I not feared Zeus, I never would have endured
such shame as this—my best friend among men
killed, and I could do nothing.
As for you, in the first place ignorance acquits you,
and then your wife, by dying, destroyed the chance   1335
to test her words, and thus convinced your mind.
You, Theseus, are the one who suffers most—
misfortune for you, but also grief for me.
The gods do not rejoice when the pious die;   1340
the wicked we destroy, children, house and all.

(Enter Hippolytus from the side, supported by attendants.)

CHORUS [*chanting*]

Here comes the suffering Hippolytus,
his fair young body and his golden head
a battered wreck. O trouble of the house,
what double sorrow from the hand of a god   1345
has been fulfilled for this our royal palace!

HIPPOLYTUS [*chanting*]

A battered wreck of body! Unjust father,
and oracle unjust—this is your work.
Woe for my fate!   1350
My head is filled with shooting agony,
and in my brain there is a leaping fire.
Let me be!
For I would rest my weary frame awhile.
Ah, ah!

Curse on my team! How often have I fed you   1355
from my own hand—you've killed, you've murdered me!
Oh, oh!
By the gods, gently! Servants, lay hands
lightly on my wounded body.
Who is this standing on the right of me?   1360
Come lift me carefully, bear me easily,
a man unlucky, by my own father cursed
in bitter error. Zeus, do you see this,
see me that worshipped the gods in piety,   1365
me that outdid all men in purity,
see me now go to death that gapes before me;
all my life lost, and all for nothing,
labors of piety in the face of men?

[singing]

Ah, ah!
Oh, the pain, the pain that comes upon me!   1370
Let me be, let me be, wretched as I am!
May death the healer come for me at last!
You kill me ten times over with this pain.
O for a spear with a keen cutting edge   1375
to shear me apart—and give me my last sleep!
Father, your deadly curse!
This evil comes from some manslaying of old,   1380
some ancient tale of murder among kin.
But why should it strike me, who am clear of guilt?
Alas!
What is there to say? How can I painlessly shake   1385
from my life this agony? O death, black night of death,
resistless death, come to me now the miserable,
and give me sleep!

ARTEMIS

Unhappy boy! You are yoked to a cruel fate.
The nobility of your mind has proved your ruin.   1390

HIPPOLYTUS [*now speaking*]
Wait!
O divine fragrance! Even in my pain
I sense it, and the suffering is lightened.
The goddess Artemis is in this place.

ARTEMIS
She is, poor man, the dearest god to you.

HIPPOLYTUS
You see my suffering, mistress?   1395

ARTEMIS
I see it. But the law forbids my tears.

HIPPOLYTUS
Gone is your huntsman, gone your servant now.

ARTEMIS
Yes, truly: but you die beloved by me.

HIPPOLYTUS
Gone is your groom, gone your shrine's guardian.

ARTEMIS
Cypris, the worker of mischief, so contrived.   1400

HIPPOLYTUS
Alas, I know now the goddess who destroyed me!

ARTEMIS
She blamed your disrespect, hated your temperance.

HIPPOLYTUS
She is but one—yet ruined all three of us.

ARTEMIS
Yes, you, your father, and his wife, all three.

HIPPOLYTUS
Indeed I'm sorry for my father's suffering.   1405

ARTEMIS

O father, this is great sorrow for you!

He was deceived by a goddess' cunning snares.

HIPPOLYTUS

O father, this is great sorrow for you!

THESEUS

I am done for; I have no joy left in life.

HIPPOLYTUS

I sorrow for you in this more than for me.

THESEUS

Would that it was I who was dying instead of you!　　　　1410

HIPPOLYTUS

How bitter your father Poseidon's gifts, how bitter!

THESEUS

Would that they had never come into my mouth.

HIPPOLYTUS

Even without them, you would still have killed me—
you were so angry.

THESEUS

                              Gods tripped up my judgment.

HIPPOLYTUS

O, if only men might be a curse to gods!　　　　1415

ARTEMIS

Enough! Though dead, you'll not be unavenged,
Cypris shall find the angry shafts she hurled
against you shall cost her dear, and this will be
your recompense for piety and goodness.　　　　1420
Another mortal, whichever one she loves
the most, I'll punish with these unerring arrows
shot from my own hand.
　　　　To you, unfortunate Hippolytus,
by way of compensation for these ills,

I will give the greatest honors of Troezen.
Unwedded maids before the day of marriage   1425
will cut their hair in your honor. You will reap
through the long cycle of time a rich reward in tears.
And when young girls sing songs, they will not forget you,
your name will not be left unmentioned,
nor Phaedra's love for you remain unsung.   1430

(To Theseus.)

Son of old Aegeus, take your son
to your embrace. Draw him to you. Unknowing
you killed him. It is natural for men
to err when they are blinded by the gods.

(To Hippolytus.)

And you, don't bear a grudge against your father.   1435
It was your fate that you should die this way.
Farewell, I must not look upon the dead.
My eye must not be polluted by the last
gaspings for breath. I see you are near this.

HIPPOLYTUS   *(Exit Artemis.)*
Farewell to you, too, holy maiden! Go in peace.   1440
You lightly leave a long companionship.
You bid me end my quarrel with my father,
and I obey. In the past, too, I obeyed you.
Ah!
The darkness is upon my eyes already.
Father, lay hold on me and lift me up.   1445

THESEUS
Alas, what are you doing to me, my son?

HIPPOLYTUS
I am dying. I can see the gates of death.

THESEUS
And so you leave me, my hands stained with murder.

HIPPOLYTUS
No, for I free you from all guilt in this.

THESEUS
You will acquit me of blood guiltiness? 1450

HIPPOLYTUS
So help me Artemis of the conquering bow!

THESEUS
Dear son, how noble you have proved to me!

HIPPOLYTUS
Farewell to you, too, father, a long farewell! 1455

THESEUS
Alas for your goodness and your piety.

HIPPOLYTUS
Yes, pray that your trueborn sons will prove as good!

THESEUS
Dear son, bear up. Do not forsake me.

HIPPOLYTUS
This is the end of what I have to bear.
I'm gone, father. Cover my face up quickly.

THESEUS
Pallas Athena's famous city,
what a man you will have lost! Alas for me! 1460
Cypris, your evils I shall long remember.

CHORUS [*chanting*]
This common grief for all the city,°
it came unlooked for. A constant stream
of manifold tears will beat down on us;
for lamentable stories about the great 1465
affect us all the more.

(Exit all.)

TEXTUAL NOTES

(The line numbers indicated are in some cases only approximate.)

AGAMEMNON

70: Text uncertain.

84: Perhaps Clytaemestra has entered silently at this point: scholars disagree.

144: Text and interpretation uncertain.

216: Text uncertain: some editors emend to read, "it is right for them to yearn furiously for the maiden's blood."

256–57: It is unclear whether the chorus mean Clytaemestra, or themselves. When exactly Clytaemestra enters is uncertain. Some scholars think that she enters silently as early as line 84.

287: Perhaps one or more lines are missing at this point.

470: Text uncertain: possibly "crash on the towering mountains."

489–500: The manuscripts (and a few editors) assign these lines to Clytaemestra, not the chorus.

570–75: Some scholars suggest that these lines must be put into a different order and that several lines are missing here.

804: Text very uncertain; some words may be missing.

934: Text uncertain. Possibly, "I, if anyone, would have known and spoken this duty."

985: Text uncertain.

1001–7: Some words seem to be missing here, and the text is very uncertain.

1090–92: Text very uncertain.

1284: This line is transposed here (from its position between 1289 and 1290 in the manuscripts) by almost all modern editors.

1359: Text uncertain.

1447: Exact reading uncertain, but the reference to a "spicy side dish" is definite.

1474: The text is defective here.

1499: Exact text and interpretation are disputed.

1527: Exact text uncertain, but the general sense is clear.

1650-54: The assignment of speakers for each of these lines is disputed.

1657: Text uncertain.

1662: Text uncertain.

PROMETHEUS BOUND

128: The text seems to indicate that the chorus enters flying, presumably either onto the roof of the stage building or by means of some kind of "machine" (*mêchanê*) that allows them to hover in the air. Modern scholars have disagreed whether or not to take these indications literally, and if so, where and how to envisage the staging of this unparalleled aerial entry of twelve or fifteen chorus members.

283: If the chorus were hovering in the air during the opening scene, they probably depart now, to reappear at ground level at 397. It is notable that they make no contact at all with Ocean (their father) in the scene that follows now, so they are probably not present.

354: Text uncertain.

397: Presumably the chorus reenters at this point into the orchestra, from the side. See note to line 283.

410: A word or two has dropped out here; "your fall" is a modern supplement.

430: A line may be missing here.

463: "Pack saddles" is an emendation accepted by most scholars for the manuscript reading "with their bodies."

541: Text uncertain.

543: Text uncertain.

558: The phrase "with your gifts" is deleted by many editors, for the meter.

760: Text uncertain. Some editors emend to read, "Since things are truly thus, you may rejoice."

792: Some editors read instead, "crossing the waves of the sea." The "waveless sea" means the dry steppes.

848: Some editors think a line has dropped out here, in which the impregnation of Io by Zeus is mentioned as well.

860: Text uncertain. Some editors think a line has dropped out here too.

880: Text uncertain.

895: There are several textual uncertainties in this stanza, but the general sense is not in doubt.

970: A line spoken by Prometheus seems to be missing before this one.

1079: How the ending was staged—whether or not the chorus departed before Prometheus' final words and whether and how Prometheus exited—is unclear.

OEDIPUS THE KING

81: Text uncertain: possibly "be happy like his eyes, and bring us safety."

198: Text uncertain.

246-51: Some editors reject these lines, regarding them as redundant after 236-43.

293: This emendation is widely accepted for the manuscript reading "No one sees who saw it."

420-21: The precise reading and interpretation are uncertain.

425: This is the reading of the manuscripts. Some editors emend the text to read, "other evils / annihilating you together with your children."

479: Or possibly "limping on his feet."

566: This is a widely accepted emendation of the manuscript reading, which has "search for the dead man."

600: This line is deleted by some scholars as an interpolation.

623–27: Two or three lines appear to have dropped out here, as the sequence of dialogue is unsatisfactory and the sense unclear.

641: The precise reading is uncertain here.

1205: The reading and interpretation here are quite uncertain, though the general sense is clear.

1280: The precise reading here is uncertain.

1316: Text and translation uncertain.

1349–50: Some editors adopt an emendation which gives, "Curse on the shepherd who . . ."

1522–30: Some editors have rejected all these final lines, arguing that they are not written in proper Sophoclean style.

ANTIGONE

5: Text uncertain.

45: Exact text and interpretation uncertain.

572–76: The assignment of speakers in lines 572, 574, and 576 varies among the manuscripts, early printed editions, and modern editors. Some assign 572 and 574 to Antigone; some assign all three lines (572, 574, 576) to Ismene.

602: Text uncertain: "knife" (*kopis*) is a modern emendation; the manuscripts have "dust" (*konis*).

606: The exact text and sense are uncertain.

781: Possibly Creon does not go inside now but remains onstage for the chorus's song, which would be unusual but not unprecedented in Greek tragedy.

782: Text and interpretation uncertain.

882: Possibly Creon has been present onstage throughout the lyric scene that preceded: see note on 781.

882–84: Text and precise meaning uncertain.

978: Exact text and interpretation not certain.

1080–83: Some editors delete these lines, in the belief that they were added (by someone other than Sophocles) so as to remind the audience of the story of the "Successors of the Seven" (*Epigoni*). Other editors retain the lines, but suggest that a few additional lines of explanation may have dropped out between 1080 and 1081.

1301: Text and interpretation uncertain; it appears that a line is missing here as well.

HIPPOLYTUS

Characters: See textual note on line 1153.

101: An ancient papyrus reads not "before your gates, the goddess Cypris," but rather "before your gates, nearby."

103–8: The translation follows the order of these lines in the manuscripts; many editors have proposed various transpositions of them.

191–97: These lines are suspected by some scholars of being an interpolation.

601: Scholars disagree about the staging of the following scene and especially about exactly where Phaedra is during the following interchange between Hippolytus and the Nurse—they take no notice of her, but she evidently hears most or all of what they say.

626: Text uncertain. Some scholars excise lines 626–27 as an interpolation.

634–37: These lines are suspected by some scholars of being an interpolation.

663: This line is suspected by many scholars of being an interpolation.

668–79: Most medieval manuscripts assign the following short song (the antistrophe to the strophe in lines 361–72) to the Nurse, but most modern scholars prefer, as do a few manuscripts, to give it to Phaedra.

680–81: The manuscripts assign these lines to the Chorus Leader, but it is probably better to give them to the Nurse.

844: A few words are missing here.

867–68: In the manuscripts there follow two lines of which the text and meaning are quite uncertain.

871–73: The ancient commentators report that these lines were missing in some manuscripts; they are rejected by many modern scholars as an interpolation.

1050: Ancient commentators report that this line was missing in many manuscripts; it is rejected by most modern scholars as an interpolation.

1102–50: In this ode, the chorus refers to itself with the masculine gender in the first strophe and with the feminine in the first antistrophe. Scholars disagree about whom to assign the ode to: the chorus of women (to whom the manuscripts attribute it), Hippolytus' hunting companions, or both in alternation (as we have printed it here).

1123: Text uncertain.

1153: This messenger may be identical with the old servant who spoke with Hippolytus at lines 88–120.

1462–66: Some scholars suspect these final lines of being due to a later author.